The Way Out

Hilaire Belloc

The Way Out

Introduction by Robert Phillips

CATHOLIC AUTHORS PRESS

Hartford, Connecticut

These essays were first published as a series of articles from February to August 1938 in the newspaper *Social Justice*, published by Social Justice Publishing Corp., Royal Oak, Michigan.

Catholic Authors Press
www.CatholicAuthors.org

ISBN: 978-0-9789432-0-2

Library of Congress Control Number: 2006933850

Contents

Introduction

In 1938 Hilaire Belloc wrote the following brilliant essays entitled "The Way Out." Although Belloc published many defenses of his economic theory known as Distributism, these essays are a marvel of clarity and succinctness containing a summary and defense of Belloc's views.

Distributism is a Twentieth Century application of traditional Catholic economic teaching of which a brief recap is in order. The Church has drawn upon two traditions of thought regarding the question of property — natural law and scripture. With respect to natural law, Aristotle rejects Plato's idea that property should be held in common by correctly arguing that property has important moral advantages. First, it increases care of property. If I personally own something, I am likely to take much better care of it than if it is part of a common store or if I rent it from a private owner. This is because I have a duty of special care which no one else specifically has. Secondly, property enhances freedom.

Wealth multiplies choices. Thirdly, property establishes an occasion for the practice of the virtue of charity. If I have nothing to share or to give others, how can I be charitable? To these we may add the Christian emphasis on charity and upon seeing to the material well being of neighbor. In traditional Catholic thinking, the family is the fundamental unit of society — it should be the focus of both productivity and reproductivity, hence, the fundamental gift of property should especially be concentrated in the family. All of these things are certainly part of Belloc's thinking, the last one in particular.

Belloc understood with great clarity that the fundamental role of the family in society is incompatible with absolutist ideologies that run roughshod over family integrity. Specifically, rigid capitalism which subordinates the individual to market forces, which undermines tradition, and which disrupts the order of family life by requiring the breadwinner to be absent from the family for most of the working week. Rigid capitalism also maintains a monopoly of property requiring what Belloc calls wage slavery.

The equally unsatisfactory reaction to rigid capitalism was socialism which was also an absolutist ideology which is immensely destructive on family life. It denies the fundamental sanctity of the family by destroying the idea of private property. Property, as we have seen, is necessary to obtain a minimal order of freedom and autonomy. In both rigid capitalism and communism autonomy is destroyed. The individual is made entirely subservient to economic forces beyond his control.

INTRODUCTION

Now it must not be assumed that Belloc is championing some kind of libertarian individualism. On the contrary, it is in the community of family and Church that the individual receives fulfillment. These are natural communities. One devoted to procreation and the other devoted to ultimate truth. It is the dialectic between these that forms the fundament of the social order.

As is well known, Belloc reached back into Medieval history to restore the concept of the guild in which individuals associated with a particular trade or profession would cooperate in the production of wealth under the overall mantle of the Catholic faith. Rigid capitalism and socialism represent an abrupt break with the continuity of Christian tradition. They are enlightenment solutions imposed upon what should have been natural evolution of Christian economic theory and practice.

The standard modernist reaction to Distributism is to say that interesting as it is, it is entirely impractical and unworkable under modern economic conditions. With the decline of communism we see that Belloc was certainly correct in predicting the impossibility of a system of pure common ownership. We now have a form of capitalism which is still profoundly unacceptable in Bellocian terms.

However, current economic developments suggest that Belloc's views have become highly relevant. In the first instance, the distribution of property in industrialized countries has becomes almost absurdly unbalanced with the 4 percentile wealthy group accumulating an almost undreamed amount of wealth. Salaries of executives of major companies have increased thousands of percentage points over the wages of ordinary workers. This is precisely what Belloc did predict. Namely, the increased concentration of wealth in fewer and fewer hands under a system of wage slavery. So in this instance, we may turn to seriously examine Belloc's views.

At the same time, the mass of workers are being relieved of even more autonomy. Personal debt, especially to credit cards, is at an out-of-control level in the search simply to make ends meet. People are now going deeply into debt just to buy groceries and other necessaries of life. When we discover that the largest employer in the United States is Wal-Mart whose wages and benefits do not even approach the possibility of supporting a family, we begin to see the outlines of Belloc's objections. Not only are Americans wage-slaves, but something which Belloc could never have even remotely imagined, the fact that not only is the father, the head-of-the-house, required to be a wage slave, but now, the mother, the heart-of-the-family, is also required to leave her children and enter the work force. Certainly, Belloc would have regarded this development as demonic.

Perhaps the picture is not entirely gloomy. Many young families are rebelling against this system of wage slavery and are going back to the land to live in relative poverty. Others are utilizing the possibilities of the Internet to found home businesses which gives them a large degree of independence while working from inside the family unit. So perhaps there

INTRODUCTION

are possibilities and signs that will emerge which are yet unknown to us. But in the end Belloc remains a beacon of
good sense directing us to the way out.

Robert Phillips
University of Connecticut

The Way Out

Chapter One

To Begin With

When a man suffers injustice he will combat with all his strength the evil done to him. This is so evident that men have in all times and places made laws, and set up tribunals, in order to enforce justice and thus prevent conflict.

When the sense of an injustice done to them is aroused in great numbers of men, there is peril of general conflict. When that sense is acute and extends to the masses of the state, all social order is threatened, and, unless the wrong be righted a whole civilization may perish.

That is the situation we have reached today in the old and the new world alike. Very great and increasing numbers of citizens feel that grievous injustice is done them by the social arrangements under which they live. This injustice they feel to be intolerable. Hence there is peril, for all the work of the world cannot be done in such an atmosphere. The strain is deathly. Unless it is relieved it will destroy us. Such is the first, the most immediate, business at hand. But there is another and a deeper consideration. Justice is of the nature things. It is the Will of the Creator, and those who resist that Will are broken at last. Order is not the end of social life. Order through Justice is the end of social life. Only in Justice can the souls of men repose. Therefore, apart from the immediate danger to be met there is a permanent solution to be sought and established. We seek Justice not only, nor even mainly, because we ourselves suffer from its absence, but because, when very many other suffer so, their strong grievance poisons the moral air we breathe. A common fundamental duty lies upon all men today, to examine, to understand, to deal with and to redress the iniquity of our time.

Here are four tests: to examine the injustice complained of (that is, to seek its cause); by such examination to understand its nature; having so understood it to work actively upon the problem presented; lastly, to do so with the object of a permanent solution. Society has fallen into a tangle through the prolonged action of unjust principles, its disease is the fruit of a false philosophy and wrongdoing — mainly through greed. When a man is presented with a tangled skein, apparently hopeless, what does he do? He first looks at the confusion closely, following up the threads until he understands the manner in which they are involved. Then he acts, pulling at the right strands in the right direction until the whole is unraveled. He has reduced chaos to order. So ought we to do, and the articles to which this is the introduction are written for that end. Society has lost the trail in the night. It has blundered into a place of mortal peril. We must find a way out.

The sense of injustice, now almost universal, is most violent in the factory and in transport, but in varying degrees it is present everywhere; and that sense of injustice is sound; for Justice demands human conditions of life for human beings — "Our Daily Bread." This is not mere sustenance; it is human dignity, it is a certain proportion of leisure, it is the enjoyment of beauty, and something more, (continually forgotten) *variety*. All these can be had under subjection to the advantage of other men, but they are then all imperfect, warped, stunted and diseased for one thing is lacking; and that one thing is freedom. The Will of Man is created free and must be exercised, if man is to live a life fully human. Choice of occupation and of things is part of "Daily Bread." Today most men have no such choice, and go hungry for it. Their lives are ordered in spite of them, and that, for one reason only: they do not possess the soil or the unencumbered instruments of their trade. Another possesses them, and through his possession and their indigence arises this bitter sense of oppression.

To the question "Why do men suffer thus?" the common answer is that the cause of all the evil is "capitalism": that is, the exploitation of the destitute many by the few who control the means of livelihood. That the answer is misleading. It states the fact but does not explain it. It is also a half-truth, and half-truths are the most dangerous falsehoods. If it were true that capitalism was the source of our evils, the destruction of capitalism, no matter how, would suffice as a remedy. But it should evident that an attempt to destroy capitalism by a wrong method is no remedy. To a man with a toothache the whole cause of his troubles seems to be the teeth in his head, but it is no remedy to cut off his head. The real cause of our troubles is not capitalism but the condition on which capitalism depends: *the destitution of the many*.

Yes! What is too learnedly called "the proletariat." But what our fathers more simply and rightly called "General Destitution" is the root evil. If we must have long words and "isms," then let us talk less of capitalism and more of "proletarianism."

Men cannot live as free citizens, capable of free contract, enjoying economic liberty, feeling their lives secure, unless they have property. By such laws as shall put property into many hands, until at least a *determining* number of citizens *own,* can society be saved. In no other way can it be saved, unless we call a return to slavery salvation.

The family is the true unit of the state, and is more important than the state. The state exists for the family, not the family for the state. Property is necessary for its normal and healthy being.

Men labor for sustenance and produce sustenance with certain instruments. Over those instruments they who labor should have control, that is, property.

Some activities function best — or can only function — in large groups. In these cases there may be shareholding — but the shares held as property. When monopoly is inevitable, by all means let it be controlled by the state, but first be certain that it is inevitable, and if you find it rising as an artificial growth, cut it down at once. A society built on ownership and therefore on freedom, with ownership safeguarded by corporate rules, will restore to us our "Daily Bread" which we have lost. Immediate necessities must be relieved for the moment; but our aim should be a stable society in a contented world. How that may be reached is the subject of what follows.

Chapter Two

The Problem Stated

The problem with which we are faced is as follows: citizens politically free and politically equal do not possess the means of livelihood. The reserves of food and of clothing, of housing, of fuel and the rest, without which human life cannot be conducted, are in the possession of, and under the control of, men different from and much smaller in number than, the mass of citizens.

It is the mass of citizens who must do the work whereby their livelihood is produced. Yet the mass of citizens are dispossessed in great areas of the world and particularly in those countries under what is called "capitalist organization." The mass of citizens are the proletarians. Such of them as can be kept alive by the minority (whose motive in keeping them alive is to make profit out of their labor) have subsistence, though no proper security of that subsidence, and no voice in what shall be made nor any property in what they make. Meanwhile a margin for whom work cannot be found would starve to death were they not artificially supported by public funds under public officials.

The free and equal citizen has political freedom, he has not economic freedom. Such a state of things cannot endure.

Let us be clear on the two essential parts of this state of affairs: citizenship and destitution. Citizens without property, citizens with no safeguard for their livelihood, men politically free but deprived of economic freedom, suffer the intolerable situation we must set right.

Where men are not free, where, by the whole organization of society, they are compelled to labor, where they are defined by law as slaves, they have a heavy grievance indeed. But they are not citizens. They are not conscious of an intolerable contrast between their admitted rights and their actual conditions. It is when the free man, the citizen, is reduced to economic subjection under other free men, that an impossible stat of affairs arises. "You say I am free? And yet I cannot even live save by your leave! You say I am free? All your laws proclaim it, it is my proudest boast; yet I may not possess the thing which I make with my own labor! You say I am free? Yet the hours in which I am to work, and the conditions under which I have to work are imposed upon me by others. You say I am free? Yet the product of my labor does not belong to me, it belongs to another, for whose advantage I am constrained to drudgery. You say I am free? Yet I cannot choose what I will consume save within very narrow limits. I must take what is presented to me by a system of production which I did not create and which is indifferent to my desires.

You say I am free and equal with my fellows? But in practice I am in thrall to those who hold that whereby men live: machines and the soil and the raw material and the necessary reserves of food and clothing and the rest which men called my equals have in their control and which I have not."

A free man, finding himself in such circumstances necessarily becomes a rebel, it is the contrast between freedom and unfree conditions of life which has set up the intolerable conditions of the modern state. That is the main problem stated in simplest terms.

necessity of REBEL

Almost in living memory the mass of men lived in houses which were their own, produced food and clothing and the rest from land which was their own, possessed the fruits of their toil, decided what they would produce and what they would consume. Within living memory there still remained so large a proportion of men whose political freedom corresponded to an economic freedom that the old tradition survived. A society in which free men owned their farms, their stores, their blacksmith's forges, their fishing craft, their carpenter shops and the rest, still continued though it was threatened and diminishing. Today the disproportion between the man economically free and the man economically unfree has grown so hugely as to throw the whole state out of balance. To restore the balance is the chief task before us.

Such is the main problem. There run intermixed with it and necessarily produced by it, other disadvantages: monotony of work which is not chosen by the worker; monotony

of produce into which craftsmanship does not enter; insta-
bility of every kind, insecurity and insufficiency. Vast numbers of men lacking proper sustenance and yet vaster numbers
lacking all certitude for the morrow. There has grown up
also a control over all human activities, by what we call
"finance" — the reign of usury and of debt, again, great
numbers of men working for the profit of the few are a con-
tradiction of what useful labor should be. It has become of
advantage to the worker to produce as little as possible for as
short a time as possible, at as high a cost as possible. It has
become of advantage to the actual producer of wealth to
check and diminish or extinguish the production of wealth.
We see that deadly paradox at work on every side.

Worst of all, perhaps, there has grown up that habit of
destitution, that loss of the sense of ownership and of real
responsibility through freedom, which we call the "proletarian mind." With each of these points I will deal in their turn,
but let us begin with the statement of the problem in its major form: we have fallen into a state where free men, equal
citizens, are, in the mass, destitute, wholly dependent upon a
minority of their more fortunate fellows, and in acute antag-
onism. It cannot go on.

Chapter Three

The Wage Worker

Disappearance of Human Relation
Hurts Both Worker and Employer

The wage worker is one who works not for himself but for
another at a wage, paid him by that other. Whether you call it
a wage or a salary, whether the wage be large or small, the es-
sence of wage-working is that the worker does not retain the
product of the work done by him. That product belongs to
another, his paymaster. And the motive of that paymaster is
to enjoy the difference between the product of the work and
the amount he has given to the worker for doing it. This difference is called "profit."

William owns a number of trees. John cuts and stacks
that lumber for a hundred dollars paid him by William. The
wood, cut, stacked and ready for use, is worth a hundred and
twenty dollars, and belongs to William. William has a profit
of twenty dollars made. Not by his labor. But by John's. Were
there not, on the average and in the long run, a profit thus

made by William out of John's labor, William would not continue to hire John.

In the beginning of such an arrangement there is no injustice. Both citizens are free men. Each enters into a free contract with the other to their mutual advantage. William owns the trees and a store of money. John wants money and engages to cut down William's trees, saw the logs and pile them up for some of William's money. The whole affair is a contract, and where citizens are free, the state enforces contracts because if it did not do so society could not go on. Only communists or despotic states can do without contract. The state, through its courts of law and its armed forces and police, enforces contacts made and, as the party to the contract are free men who voluntarily bound themselves, neither of them can complain or has any grievance against the other.

Yet when we look around on the modern world we see millions of wage-earners in a white heat of anger against the owners of capital who provide their wages and the instruments wherewith they work. The anger is so great that it continually leads to physical conflict inspired by a burning sense of injustice. This anger has lead, over and over again, to rioting, and to massacre. The strain gets worse everywhere, the disturbances increase with it, and it is beginning to look as though, unless we can settle the quarrel, society will go to pieces.

Why did wage-working, which began as a just and reasonable arrangement become intolerable?

THE WAGE WORKER

The reason is that things can change their character when they change their scale. Fifty or sixty pedestrians walking up and down the street, each engaged on his own affairs, are something utterly different from six thousand men roaring down the street together, all engaged on the same object. The first is a peaceable, everyday happening; the second is a dangerous mob breaking into riot.

So it has been with the wage-worker. So long as most citizens owned land and instruments and house-room, and the rest, then it was a natural contract for one man to take wages from another. The wage-worker might himself be an owner, adding to his income for the moment by a particular bit of work; or if he saved on his wages he could become an owner. The number of wage-workers working for one particular man was small. The relations between the citizen who paid the wage and the citizen who earned it was personal and human. But when, under the action of competition and the use of expensive and centralized machines, and rapid communication, you have thousands of men working at a wage under one paymaster or corporation, things are utterly changed — and that is where we stand today. Our industrial society has become divided into a very large body which lives wholly, or almost wholly, on wages, that is on food, clothing and housing, doled out to it at short intervals by a much smaller number of paymasters, who control capital: that is, stores and reserves of land, housing, clothing and food.

The human relation has disappeared, you have the naked contrast between an employing class exploiting a vastly

human relationship gone

15

larger employed class for profit. The interests of the two are directly hostile. The wage-worker is the enemy of the pay-master. It is the business of the paymaster to give the wage earner as little as possible, and to make him work as hard as possible for that little. It is the business of the wage-worker to work, and therefore to produce, as little as possible for as much as he can get out of the paymaster. The whole scheme of wealth production becomes irrational and topsy-turvy. The paymasters, who direct, do not aim at wealth produc-tion — which serves us all — but at their own profit. The wage-worker does not aim at wealth production by his work, but on the contrary, at working as little as possible for the largest pay.

Meanwhile, every sort of social abomination arises from this evil root. There is the spiritual abomination of what is called "Class Hatred," the oppressed hating the oppressor. There is the corresponding spiritual abomination of con-tempt, injustice and falsehood. The secure oppressor de-spises the wage-earner, does him the injustice of using labor without thought of the wage-earner's advantage or of the community, and he tells a falsehood that was a truth at the beginning of the affair but is now a lie: he says that all this is based on free contract and is therefore rightly en-forced by the courts of law and the armed services of the community.

There you have the plain statement of the monstrous evil we are out to remedy. In order to remove it we must look closely at each bad fruit growing on that bad tree.

There is the bad fruit of insufficiency for the mass of men living on a wage, which it is the interest of the paymaster to make as small as possible: insufficiency for masses of those who get work and desperate conditions for those who do not.

There is insecurity for millions of men uncertain how long the food and housing and clothing of their families will be provided.

I will take these two evils in my next two articles, one after the other.

Chapter Four

Insufficiency and Insecurity

When the system of wage working began to be fully developed under what is called "industrial capitalism," it became more and more evident that the increasing mass of wage-workers would suffer from insufficiency, because the driving force of the system was the making of profit and, therefore, the paying as little as possible for labor. When the wage-worker had no other resources, he had to take what was given him and his paymaster gave him as little as possible. The masses suffered insufficiency of food, bad housing conditions, poor clothing and the rest of it. This was first apparent in England, where the new wage working system was born. Wherever industrial capitalism arose elsewhere in Europe, the same conditions of insufficiency followed it.

The evil did not spread to America till much later, because in America there was a vast reserve of undeveloped land and natural resources. Also in America, for a long time, a large proportion of the wage workers had the chance of changing their condition by moving to new undeveloped places and, even if they remained at a wage, selling their labor at a good price because it was in high demand. But even the United States at last began to feel the growth of the evil. Insufficiency, a natural fruit of production for profit, pressed everywhere upon the masses of society.

To meet this the workers organized themselves. They struck collective bargains with their paymasters, using the weapon of the strike to enforce their demands. The consequence was a state of continuous social warfare throughout industrial society. Moreover, as the interests of the worker at a wage and of the controller of capital were directly opposed, this warfare not only embittered relations throughout the whole community, but lowered the economic value of the community. One hostile body, the employers, did all they could to lower the wage and therefore the purchasing power of the other hostile body opposed to it, the wage workers. That other hostile body did all it could to diminish the profit, that is, to weaken the motive force of production.

Meanwhile, there was always a large margin of workers who could not find employment. In times of economic stress this margin became enormous. It was always a vile thing that many should be without resources; when the number passes a certain level it became a mortally perilous thing. America, which had long offered special advantages to the wage-workers, and had maintained a large proportion of free citizens not dependent on a wage, was flooded with immigrant workers from overseas; the wage-earners began to be the larger part of the citizens and, in the towns, the mass of their population.

When this state of things had established itself in America as in Europe, the whole of our civilization where it was industrialized had fallen into a hopeless tangle. The organization of the wage earners at high wages choked production and at the same time there went along with it, to one side of it, the growth of vast bodies of men unemployed, or employed at a grossly insufficient wage.

On the top of this there was the insecurity of all wage earners, even the best paid. Every man dependent on a wage knew it might at any moment fail him.

The unemployed were not even a permanent body. Nearly the whole of the wage-earners had either experience of unemployment at some time of their lives or the threat of it hanging over them. Insufficiency and insecurity had become the marks of all those who labored in the industrial world. But the two things necessary to the human family on the material side are sufficiency of livelihood and security therein. Lacking these, through some machinery of social justice, men cannot bear the conditions under which they live.

Attempts were made in some countries, where the deadlock had become impossible, to apply temporary remedies, especially to the evil of insecurity. Industrial Germany led the way in this, almost a lifetime ago. England, where the need was more desperate, was compelled to follow suit. Sums were raised by compulsion: partly from the general taxpayer, partly out of wages, partly by a special levy on employers, to insure the workers against unemployment and to maintain them where the sums they received were insufficient to meet the lowest standards of life. The wage-earners were relieved of one small burden after another, they were given small pensions in old age, their expenses were paid during sickness, the teaching of their children was met out of public funds, temporary laws were even passed to reduce their rents, that is, to take away part of the house-owner's property, for the advantage of the poor tenant.

But all these were evidently no more than what are called "palliatives." So long as a great number of citizens in some countries, the great bulk of citizens, were at once free and deprived of property, the root of the evil remained untouched. The evil tree was not cut down, it would continue to bear its evil fruits.

Since the two conditions which combined to create such calamities were freedom and destitution, many began to propose that freedom should be sacrificed. It was the line of least resistance. But of that I shall treat later when I come to talk of communism. the obvious immediate remedy was worse than the disease.

While the worker at a wage thus suffered, what was left of small ownership was suffering also. The free man who still owned was more and more threatened with loss of ownership.

Chapter Five

The Ruin of the Small Owner

Mass Production Has Ousted Free
Craftsmen, But He Can Still be Saved

Our fathers rightly thought of a free society as being made up of men economically free. One can only be fully free if he owns the means by which one lives. These owners who made up the bulk of the old society, before Industrial capitalism and Big Business arrived, were what we call today "small owners." Suppose that out of ten families in the community seven were farmers tilling their own land, there would be difference in the amount of land each family had and difference in its fertility, in the value of their interments and livestock and houses. The average would be less than the wealth of the most conspicuous among them. That is why we call an average ownership of this kind "small ownership"; not that it is too small to provide a decent livelihood but that it is small compared with the more conspicuous larger ownerships. Now this small owner, a typical citizen of a free and contented state, is rapidly disappearing in our evil modern conditions and looks like being wiped out altogether. He is being changed from a free man into a man only half free: a proletarian wage-worker. That is the central social misfortune of our time. The small owner is on the way to ruin.

This has come about through the isolation of the small owner; he stands unprotected against forces hostile to his existence. Whether he be the small free owning farmer, or the small free craftsman, carpenter, smith or whatnot, owning his own home and shop and tools, his numbers are rapidly getting less and we are making for his extinction.

Remark, to begin with, that a man is not a free owner if he is encumbered with debt. The man to whom he owes the debt has, to that extent, taken over part of his ownership. If that debt bears interest, as all modern debt does, he is not only the less of an owner by the amount of the debt, but always may be and often is eaten up by the accumulation of these payments.

But even the unencumbered small owner is today the prey of hostile forces which are destroying him. He has to sell the produce of his labor in a market of which he knows hardly anything compared with what is known by the large operator; he has, therefore, on occasion to sell suddenly at a ruinous loss. He has only a few kinds of things to sell, so he cannot "spread over" his gains and losses. For the transport of his produce to the consumer he is dependent upon great organizations over which he has no control and with whom whatever contract he makes is one heavily weighted against him. He has only small reserves, if any, to fall back upon. He is more and more dependent for his power to carry on at all upon credit extended to him by money lenders, that is, by the banking system. But even where credit would save him he has far less opportunity to get it than has the big man and gets it on far less favorable terms. In every form of competition the small owner carries a heavy handicap, as things are today.

Another force hostile to his survival is that the cost of novel and more efficient instruments of production, sometimes the actual instrument of production, the machine to be used is a much larger unit than the old-fashioned one; it costs more than the small owner can afford. This is notably the case in all metalcraft and wood-work, as it is also in building. Very often, careful individual work is in competition with mass-production which can only be done cheaply if it is done on a very large scale, altogether beyond the powers of the small man; boot and shoe making are a conspicuous example of this. Sometimes the new and more efficient instrument is neither larger nor more expensive than the old-fashioned instrument, but even then the small man has to stand the burden of scrapping the old instrument and buying a new one, and that burden is far heavier for him than for the big man.

In all these ways is the small owner being attacked and the attack is far stronger than the defense. Vast manufactories for the production of metal-ware have ousted the smith.

Mass production of furniture has ousted the independent free cabinet-maker. Combinations of steam craft, whole fleets of them, are ousting the free fisherman, the owner of his own boat. In England this last tragedy has been worked out in my own lifetime and before my own eyes. Small transport has been killed by the larger steamer, and of course, on land, still more effectively by the universal development of railways.

It was hoped that perhaps electricity, and later the motor car and the internal combustion engine, would restore the small man; and they could have done so; but great combinations of capital were too strong for him.

He is certainly in peril of death. Is he then doomed, as nearly all men take it now for granted that he is?

I do not think so. I think he can be saved and restored, or at any rate that his economic freedom can be.

But of that later. We must talk next of the fellow to the small owner, the small distributor, the small storekeeper who is in an equally bad way; and is thought, by most people around us, to be doomed even more certainly than his brother, the small owner.

There are those who think they can save the small owner; but hardly anyone thinks we can save the small storekeeper.

Let us see.

Chapter Six

The Ruin of the Small Storekeeper

Thousands of Independent Dealers Now
Work as Managers for a Small Salary

The phrase "small distributor" is a pompous but accurate way of saying "small storekeeper." He also was an economically free man as was the unencumbered farmer of his own land. The small storekeeper was an independent citizen under no master. He is threatened with disappearance like his brother the small owner: the craftsman, the farmer. He is more menaced than the small owner and is in danger of disappearing altogether sooner even than the small owner will.

There are two sets of causes for his misfortune. A moral set and a material set.

On the moral side, there is the lack of natural excuse for, and natural sympathy with, the small distributor as compared with the small craftsman or farmer. The craftsman or farmer produces directly things which are necessary to our lives: food and clothing and furniture and the rest. When we think of him, we think of work necessary and useful for everybody. But the storekeeper is only a middleman. He passes on what the small owner has made or, nowadays, what the big manufactory has made, to the consumer; and there is no apparent natural argument for this function of "passing on the goods" being in the hands of small business more than big business. Indeed, if we could get the necessaries of life direct, without having recourse to middlemen at all, we should think it a good thing.

Then there is the fact that the wage-earners have no special sympathy with the small storekeeper. Some few of them may have the sense to feel rather vaguely that they are all in the same boat together against the big capitalists. But the wage earning masses will buy what they need wherever they can get it cheapest and do not trouble particularly about supporting the small dealer.

As for the wealthier people, they find the small storekeeper inconvenient, compared with the large store. It seems to them squalid, compared with the comfort and luxury to which they are accustomed, and it is necessarily less able to provide at a moment's notice what they happen to want.

Now this last point: the opinion of the wealthier people is very important, for they have a great deal to do with the making of general opinion.

So much for the moral forces working against small business. The material forces are even stronger. You have among these material forces some that are working against small business for the same reason that they are working against small ownership. Small business has less information than big business. It has less variety or perhaps none, selling only one thing, where the big store sells a number of different things, therefore it cannot make up for loss on one kind of sales by profits on another. It has no "spread over." Then again, like small ownership, small business has less command of credit than large business. Very often the bank will not listen to it at all and when it does it changes more in proportion for a small loan than it does for a large one.

In all these ways small business is handicapped in its struggle to live, precisely as small ownership is handicapped.

But there are also special enemies to small distributors which attack them as distributors and from which the small owner is free.

Big business has proportionately smaller "overhead" than small business, even the rent it pays is often heavier *in proportion to the turn-over* than the rent paid by the big stores; while the clerical expenses and pretty well all the running expenses are proportionately heavier.

Then there is the cost of advertisement, which has become so enormously important in modern capitalist distribution. A hundred thousand dollars spent in a given time on large advertisements has far more than a hundred times the effect of a thousand spent on petty advertisement. In practice, small business hardly advertises at all, while big business shouts at us everywhere.

Then there is the giving of contracts. For instance, in the catering trade. A big catering firm will get the order for banquets for the feeding of great numbers of men in institutions, or the armed forces; a small catering firm will not, and a little store can never find anything of the sort coming its way.

Then there is the extra cost of supply; small business has to pay far more in proportion for getting its petty stock delivered to it than has big business.

Meanwhile, every added facility for rapid transport and rapid communication of orders, increases the power of the chain stores. So all along the line. Under free competition small business goes to the wall. The small distributor is sinking fast. The human instinct for independence desperately maintains his hopeless struggle, but hopeless it is as things are, and he is going under.

All the observers in his own line of life, especially the big distributors, see this clearly. It is most instructive to listen to the conversation of big business men on the shortcomings and misfortunes of the old fashioned single storekeeper. The newspaper (with whom the small man cannot advertise) are equally certain of his doom.

Now, as in the case of the small owner, the loss of economic independence means that the man and his family become proletarian.

A friend in the trade assures me that within his own lifetime some forty thousand independent grocers in one European country are now replaced by four thousand salaried managers living on a wage, the servants of one big company and at its mercy. This flood of proletarianism grows and grows, and with it there comes to clog the whole community what may be called "the proletarian mind." *This proletarian mind is, as I have said, the real danger of our time.* capitalism is but a product thereof.

Chapter Seven

The Proletarian Mind

*When a Man's Work Enriches Not Himself
But Another, Work Appears an Evil Thing*

The small owner of old days — farmer, craftsman, boat-owner, storekeeper — was a fully free man.

He possessed the instruments of his livelihood, no one could take them away and so take away his livelihood with them. He thought as a free man he estimated his well-being in terms of property. He did not think of property as the privileges of a few, or as an unfair advantage; he thought of it as a natural condition of life, enjoyed by most citizens. He inherited property — especially his house and land. He left it to his children. When he made a contract freely with another free man, he felt bound to observe that contract and felt it no grievance that the other party should require him to do so. He took his share of the public burden, paying, out of his own money, certain sums for public purposes: in those days sums small compared with his total earnings. It was natural that he should help to decide with his fellows how public funds thus formed should be spent. So the whole democratic system could work easily and well.

His labor enriched him. It paid him to be a hard worker. If he was slack in his work he was blameworthy, not only in the eyes of his neighbor, but in his own eyes. Such men forming the most part of the commonwealth gave society its tone and spirit. Those who were not owners could become so by saving and, after serving other men, could become independent in their turn.

Society was inspired politically by the Free Mind, which is in harmony with man's nature: for all men have Free Will.

But when this free man sank to be a proletarian, deprived of property, wholly dependent upon a wage, his mind gradually changed. At last he became a man with a *proletarian mind*. To the *proletarian mind* work is evil, a burden wrongfully imposed by another.

The proletarian knows that his work enriches not himself but somebody else. He cannot, by saving, in a proletarian society acquire independence as a small owner; for in a proletarian society the small owner is ruined. An exceptional man can rise out of the proletariat into the privileged owning class, but he does so at the expense of his fellows. The mass of him can never be other than proletarian, or at least the proletarian mind gets into that mood and is fixed in it.

The proletarian mind feels every incentive to spending what it earns and no incentive to saving, just as it has no direct incentive to work save for the necessity of keeping alive: and livelihood which is, in social justice, no more than his due, is not the product of his own choice and effort, but is doled out to him by another.

His ideal can only be to get as much as possible for as little effort as possible. In pursuing that ideal his capitalist master sets him the example; for the owners who in a capitalist state (that is, a proletarian society) are a privileged minority. They live by profit and by obtaining as much as possible for as little effort as possible — often with no effort beyond the gambler's effort.

The proletarian mind is not conscious of duties to the commonwealth, save, still, in one particular, that of patriotism; and even that is growing weaker with the proletariat as proletarian conditions grow more hopelessly permanent.

Far worse spiritual consequences follow. The proletarian mind loses the sense of home. For a proletariat has no roots. It drifts from place to place. Its habitation is "the labor market." It inherits nothing and has no hope of handing on anything to posterity. To tell the plain truth, the proletarian mind despairs. So do the minds of its masters, for the evil we do to others bears fruit in ourselves.

The proletarian mind cannot but fall into hatred of its oppressor and that hatred is enhanced by the contempt of which it feels itself to be unjustly the victim.

In such a mood how is it possible for men to enjoy leisure, to keep their sense of beauty and to exercise the Arts? The whole thing is inhuman.

Meanwhile the privileged owners live in dread of falling into the proletarian condition. That catastrophe lies before them on every occasion and this dread affects especially those who think wrongfully to benefit by the sufferings of their fellow men.

The proletarian mind easily adheres to the profession of democracy. It will acclaim leaders who talk of democracy. But it is incapable of democratic action. It has forgotten what it was to be free. That is why modern industrial capitalism, as it is called (but we know that its true name is "proletarianism") more and more in one country after another accepts a despot and under whatever name the despot is labeled looks to it for salvation from its misery.

There has never been such a mood before in the history of the world and of it nature it cannot endure, but in passing it may breed something worse still. Never before has there been a social system based upon destitution combined with political freedom; upon free citizens lacking economic freedom.

Note particularly that the worst feature in the whole affair is the lack of human bonds. To a man who has not experience of anything but the modern social injustice and who is filled with bitterness, the strength and value of a human bond, of loyalty, affection, neighborly custom between the poorer and the wealthier man can mean nothing. But to those who have experience of such human bonds, they mean everything.

It is not too late now to attempt a restoration of the old loyalties and personal contacts and long domestic familiarity which humanized and modified and made tolerable the older inequalities among men. When we come to speak of restoring better things we shall not begin by taking the proletarian mind for granted, we shall rather begin by aiming at destroying that mind and substituting for it conditions of economic freedom and the free mind of the free man.

Chapter Eight

Usury

I now go on to talk of the plague of monopoly, which is one of the very worst results of modern capitalism, and is ruining society quite as much as the burning sense of injustice suffered by the worker under capitalism. I shall speak of the monopoly of production gradually killing men's choice of where they shall buy and of whom; the virtual monopoly of credit, through the concentration of banking and the stranglehold of the bankers on the modern capitalistic world.

But before we can understand the growing monopoly of credit we must understand *usury*.

First, let us understand what we are talking about. The word "usury" is used today in two very different senses. It is used to mean excessive interest on money: that is the popular meaning of the word. It is also used to mean *interest on money as distinguished form profit: any interest,* large or small, demanded for the "use of money" as distinguished from payments for goods or services and from profit on trade. This is the strict original meaning of the word "usury" and in that sense I use it here: interest on money or credit alone.

It is a strange thing that though usury has been denounced as an accursed sin, a destruction of society, ever since human history has existed, it has in modern times been left alone, and, until quite lately, was not seriously discussed. It was taken for granted that usury was quite natural and would do no harm. The ancient pagan philosophers denounced it; the Christian Church denounced it vigorously from the appearance of this Church until the Reformation. All our moral theologians have denounced it. And yet, for a time, after the seventeenth century, until quite recently, usury was more and more accepted until it became a matter of course. Only when the enormous harm that it had done was beginning to be felt was the question raised again.

Now, usury being the taking of interest on money merely *as money*, why is that wrong and harmful? Money is a social instrument devised for the exchange of goods. Its proper function is to work as currency. It does not breed. There is no natural profit attaching to it merely as money. If you keep it back from general circulation and take advantage of having it thus in your power and say to man who needs to buy or sell, "You shall not have this necessary currency unless you pay me still more money for the use of it" you are doing wrong.

The principle of taking usury once admitted, usury would end by eating up society. A few dollars lent out at compound interest for a few generations would demand a tribute more than all the wealth of the world could meet. A sum of money lent at 5 percent doubles, at compound interest, in just over 14 years. The debt increases a *thousandfold* in 144 years; in 288 years a *millionfold!* In 432 years a *billionfold!* — one thousand million times! One cent put out at such interest when Columbus landed would now claim more than $200,000,000.

But, clearly you are doing no wrong if you put your wealth into some profitable enterprise and claim a portion of the profit thereon. That is where the confusion arises.

Supposing a man owns a piece of land through which, deep down, runs a rich vein of copper ore. The amount of ore that could be extracted in a year's labor would be worth, by the time he had got the ore to the surface, $100,000. But to get it to the surface needs instruments and reserves of food and clothing and housing and the rest of it to maintain human energy while the ore is being extracted.

The owner of the vein had nothing. He gets a partner with $500,000 and his partner buys the required machinery and reserves of food, etc., so that the work can be undertaken. He bargains to halve, at the end of the year, the value of the ore extracted: that is, $50,000: one-tenth of the amount that he has put up as capitol. The other $50,000 of ore is to be kept by the owner of the land. Year after year one goes on taking his share as capitalist. But the other man has the advantage of *his* share, which he could never have had without the help of his partner. The contract is perfectly just.

Now suppose after 20 years the mine peters out. There is no more profit to be shared and therefore the original contract comes to an end from lack of matter.

But supposing the contract were worded so that the capitalist did not get his 10 percent as part profit, but got it as interest on money lent: not as instruments and reserves of food, etc., lent. Then he has a perpetual claim to $50,000 a year, payable out of wealth that is not there. This is called "interest on the unproductive loan" and such interest is usury. To pay that tribute the borrower has to get further and further into debt or to sell other wealth of his, until he is ruined; and that is how usury eats up society.

Now when money claims interest *merely because it is money and without reference to the way that money is used,* a large proportion of the interest must always be interest on what has become an unproductive loan. Part of the vast sums paid to the money lenders annually represents real profit, real wealth, real goods. But part will always represent, if money lending instead of partnership is at work, interest on a loan which has become, or was from the beginning unproductive.

For instance, nearly all the great war loans demand interest on an unproductive loan. The money was spent in buying goods which were consumed, not in producing more wealth, but in producing no wealth — or even in destroying wealth. It went to support soldiers and sailors who produced no wealth and often actually destroyed wealth. It went to buy guns and ammunition which produce no wealth, but were often actively employed in destroying wealth. You spend

$100,000 in buying guns and ammunition for knocking down in war an industrial building which, in peace, produced $5,000 worth of wealth a year; and you go on asking $5,000 interest on the money represented by worn out guns, exploded ammunition and a factory that has been destroyed. There are other ways in which the recognition of money's right to interest, merely because it is money, eats up society, but this one major case of the unproductive loan is sufficient to show the evil that usury does.

When money lending ("the providing of credits" as it is called) carries interest as a matter of course, it is an activity which devours mankind.

Chapter Nine

The Disease of Monopoly

*The lack of Corporate Powers to Guarantee
the Independence of the Small Dealer Makes
Single Control Appear More Inevitable Than It Is*

When industrial capitalism arose, rather more than 100 years
ago, many foresaw its dangers. It would give economic, and
therefore political, power to the owners of the new machines
and the new system of commerce and banking. It was pointed
out that the motive for producing wealth would no longer be
the satisfying of human needs, but personal and selfish greed.
The man who control the bank or a factory or a transport
system would exploit his fellow man and exploit the public.

To this the answer was given: "The evil undone by the action of competition." To many of our fathers, to many of
our fathers — to nearly all of them at one moment — that
answer seemed sufficient.

The man who owns a bakery has got the bread, and you
cannot eat unless you buy from him, but another man owns

another bakery and the competition between them will ensure your having bread at the cheapest rate. One man controls a new railway, and you can only get to such and such a place by his leave along that railway; but another man owns another railway; the two will compete and therefore you will get there as cheaply as possible — and so on all down the list. Competition will serve the double purpose of making wealth plentiful and preventing any man or group of men, from becoming masters of all.

That argument worked until within living memory; today it has broken down. All men of my generation (I was born in 1870) remember the times when steamship lines, railways, stores, and pretty well all economic activities, though motivated by individual love of gain, were checked and made useful by active competition. This principle had the further spiritual advantage of freedom, and freedom has a spiritual advantage when it exists because it corresponds with the divinely given free will of man. Competition existed because free citizens could start what industry they liked, where they liked, buy at their own price and sell at their own price, and the ultimate result was to the good of the community, making everything cheaper and producing abundance of wealth.

But, since the principle at the root of the thing was false, it was bound to produce false results. You do not get a good result from an evil or imperfect motive. And this motive of individual gain and profit, pushed beyond a certain point, ended with the destruction of that very competition which had pleaded as its excuse for existence. It became apparent that the two bakers could combine and so control bread. It became apparent that the two competing railroads could combine and prevent your getting from one place to another save on their own terms.

What is called, today, "the merger" was born. With it was born the chain store, the department store and all the rest of it. The smaller activities were "competed" out of existence, and monopoly began to show its ugly head. A common name for it in America was "the trust." In England when it first appeared, the people who benefitted by it lied freely and pretended it was not there. But facts were too strong for them and they were found out. Nearly 40 years ago a far-seeing Englishman wrote, "England has become the home of the trust." Today this is universally true. You see it in every-thing. the English railways are virtually combined into one business, so are the banks, so are other whole departments of trade: the area of free competition becomes smaller and smaller.

This process was powerfully aided by the new inventions which made the communication of commands and the de-livery of goods more rapid. A man might acquire a monop-oly and such a trade, over such and such an area, before the telegraph and telephone. With the coming of these he could vastly extend his field of operations. The facility of commu-nication enabled him to set up his stores and managers every-where. With dominating capital he could under-sell and ruin. In the end most of the industrial activities of the com-munity, most of those which depended upon machinery in any form, had turned into what were virtually, or actually, monopolies.

When I was a boy a vast number of milk walks (as they were called in London) looked after the distribution of milk to the populace, and each made an individual living. Today you see everywhere the monogram and the authority of one great distributing company. When I was already approaching middle-age the fishmongers still were men with individual shops. Today, one great combine controls an increasing number of them in England, and what is worse, can dictate its terms to the fishermen. So it is with everything, except, as yet, the land. But even the land is now becoming subservient to capitalist machine control.

It has all happened with startling rapidity and has about it the appearance of an inevitable movement to which men must bow. That appearance is false, our fate is in our own hands. But by that appearance most people already have been deceived, and you hear on every side the plea "Since monopoly is inevitable, we must accept the tyranny of the state. The private citizen, economically free, is no longer possible." We shall see in later articles why that is false.

The disease of monopoly, which is ruining freedom, and against which nearly all men protest, and some men have the courage to act — though both the protest and the action are confused — is a main symptom of our modern mortal disease.

In some things, through the nature of the instruments employed, and even through the nature of the activity itself, monopoly is inevitable. Where it is inevitable, public control, or at least public check and supervision, is essential. But it often appears to be inevitable where it is nothing of the sort; where it has simply arisen through the lack of corporate institutions for guaranteeing the independence of the small dealer, the small producer and the small owner in general.

This disease of monopoly is apparent in many forms, but there are three in particular which immediately concern the modern world:

1. The monopoly of production and distribution, including transport,

2. The monopoly of information, and

3. The most important of all, the virtual monopoly of credit.

What that means, and how it now grasps the community, I will deal with in my next article. But first let us be perfectly clear that the word "monopoly" does not necessarily mean, used in this sense, "control by one man," or even control by one corporation. It means controlled by a number of units, insignificant compared with the total number of the community. Such units work in confederation, using means of their own over which the public has no control, and therefore holding the public in their grip.

You may say that a number of competing banks exist, and that the breakdown of so many in times of crisis is proof of freedom. You may say that side by side with the general store there is still the individual store, that new enterprises are perpetually rising up, and the small man still has a chance to make good. All that is true, but the large lines of the movement are indisputable.

Under the present system of unrestrained competition, the ownership of the means of production, transport, distribution, information and especially credit in the hands of a few, you have an increasing tendency to monopoly, and the community is subservient to monopoly.

In my next articles I shall deal with the three forms of monopoly already mentioned: Credit, Production and Distribution, Information.

Chapter Ten

Capital Kills Its Own Market

*Monopoly of Production, Distribution and
Transport Increases the Subjection of the Many to
the Will of an Exploiting Few, So That Economic
Freedom Bids Fair to Become Only a Memory.*

The growing monopoly of production of goods, and of their transport and distribution through retail trades, is familiar to all of us. We have already seen how unrestricted competition, followed by mergers, puts these affairs into fewer and fewer hands.

Consider the social effects of this: (1) It makes the total goods available arbitrary in amount, that amount being dependent upon the interest or calculations of a few controllers. Suppose an extreme case which has no actual existence, but illustrates the principle. Suppose one man in a community of 1,000,000 men controlled all the land and all the capital: that is the machinery and the reserves of seed, food, clothing, housing, etc.

It might not be to his advantage or caprice to set men to work save for satisfying his own needs. He could not send them all to work, or even most of them to work, to his advantage, though he might do so out of desire for the public good. But it may be said, he would want to sell the goods which he ordered to be produced. Whom would he sell them to? He might try to sell them abroad, with increasing difficulty, because nations are more and more keeping out foreign goods. If he sells them to his own destitute dependents they can only pay with such sums as he doles out to them.

Of course, I say again, this is only an imaginary condition. But the smaller the number of people who control production, the nearer you get in reality to this state of things.

(2) Under industrial capitalism, that is, under a state of affairs in which a few people control the system of production, and distribution and exchange, and the great mass of people are dependent on them, it pays the controllers to give the great mass of people as small purchasing power as possible. For under capitalism, production, transport, etc., go on for profit. The difference between values produced and the wage ccost of producing them is their profit, and the smaller the wage cost the greater the profit. In other words, "Capitalism kills its own home market."

Those are the two principal material disadvantages of capitalism as we now have it. They are translated, in the actual world, into the terms "Unemployment" and "Insufficient purchasing power." So long as control is in few hands and gets into fewer and fewer hands — these evils must grow larger and larger.

But the spiritual disadvantages of control by few and yet fewer men, over the process of production, transport and the rest, are even worse than the material disadvantages.

These spiritual disadvantages take three main forms. First there is loss of choice: the individual cannot exercise his free will in taking up this and that which he likes and rejecting this and that which he does not like. More and more, demand does not call forth supply, but supply imposes itself on demand. There is increasing loss of freedom in selection, and more constrained.

And the second spiritual disadvantage is the counterpart of this: an increasing uniformity in the pattern of existence. It has been well said that "multiplicity is life." When men are all getting the same sort of things turned out in the same way and on the same model by the hundred million, life loses its zest. Complete uniformity is death.

The third spiritual misfortune is this: that the mass of men fall under the will of a few. They not only fall under the will of a few controllers — called "employers" or "officials" — upon whom their wages, and therefore their very existence depends but, conversely, their own wills are gradually atrophied. That is the worst evil of all: the activity of the will is essential to the dignity of man. It is normal to man, and the rejection of it beyond a certain degree is increasingly harmful to man.

Here we ought to distinguish between two things which are often muddled together: voluntary subjection and enforced subjection. Any man choosing a profession surrenders his will in part to the rules of his profession. The sailor and soldier do it more than the civilian; those in the religious life do it most of all. But if they make that surrender of their own free will, that free will remains intact. It is otherwise when they are compelled to monotony and to dependence on the will of others.

Now, there is a last evil connected with the growing diminution in the numbers of those who control and the growing increase in the numbers of those who are dependent. That evil is perhaps the worst of all. It is the evil of bad habit.

When any bad process begins there is, in its first stages, a memory, a tradition, of better things. The old and better state of affairs still possesses what physical science calls "acquired momentum." So it is with freedom when monopoly of control is growing up. All the older people can remember real competition and a fairly good division of property. The younger people may not remember it, but they hear what their elders remember, and are still sufficiently in touch with the past to have about them the atmosphere of economic freedom, though they have lost the reality of it.

A human generation is short. When it has lost what it once knew, habit turns the new conditions into matters of course till the new conditions come to seem almost part of the universe. At last it becomes impossible for men to imagine what the older and better state of affairs was like.

Now this habit in any evil, but especially the habit of dependence, is what makes evil permanent; and as things are now going there is a rapidly increasing danger that this condition of dependence upon a few, and of accepting monopoly of control over our lives will become second nature. If we allow that to happen by allowing the gradual decay of individual property and freedom to continue unchecked, it will be impossible to return. That is the real danger when we pass the point after which reform becomes practically impossible because the mind cannot conceive it.

Here in England, where I write, we have had within my own lifetime a striking example of this. When I was young there was a strong movement still in existence for turning leaseholds into permanent property. The object was to transform men who paid rent into men who owned their houses and farms. Today the idea has almost disappeared. You get increasing numbers who are supposed to own their houses, but who as a fact, are paying tribute on loans. Their houses and land are not owned by themselves but by credit societies, and the vast majority, who do not even nominally own their houses, no longer make an effort to do so, nor ask for a reform of the law which would permit them to do so.

That is only one example. This effect of habit is to be seen on every side and if we do not bring about a reform on time, the second generation after our own will have forgotten what economic freedom is.

Chapter Eleven

The Suppressed Truth

*The Monopoly of Information Through the Power to
Control the Press and Radio Is Most Dangerous to
Society When It Is Used to Boycott Facts*

The next most important branch of modern monopoly is
monopoly of information.

As in all other forms of monopoly, there is a wide margin
still left. Information is not monopolized in the sense that it
can only be obtained from one source; but the tendency to
monopoly in it is very marked, and it is increasing under our
eyes. The importance of this tendency will escape no one.
We can make no judgment on public affairs, and very few
judgments on our own private affairs, without adequate general information. If information be withheld or warped in
the interests of those few who control it, the gravest harm is
done to the citizen and to the commonwealth.

There are three forms in which this tendency appears: (1)
What is called "the air" — it used to be called "the ether" —

that is, the wireless; radio; (2) The general journalistic press; and (3) books, with which may be counted The more instructed magazines.

The wireless tends to monopoly in two ways: first, it may be bought up by a few commercial interests which tend, like all forms of capitalist control, to get fewer and more powerful. Secondly, it may be an admitted monopoly of the government.

Of these two the latter is certainly the more dangerous and the worst. In European countries, and particularly in England, the radio is a public monopoly of this kind. It is, of course, mere hypocrisy that it is not controlled by the state. It is controlled by a corporation which the state charters, and to which the state appoints the officials. Those who prefer this form of monopoly by wireless are always pointing out the evils of the alternative system, where wireless is free to be bought by anyone who chooses to hire it. The mass of men remain, so far as the wireless is concerned, completely ignorant of whatever the government chooses to shut off from them.

The tendency to monopoly in information by newspapers is strong and dangerous, but it may be exaggerated. There are few cases in which what is called "a newspaper magnate" really controls all the printed daily information available to the public, even in a limited area. Moreover, although the man with the large numbers of newspapers under one control and distributed over vast areas has much too much power, yet there is a limit to it in another form, which is that people do not necessarily take his advice. The real danger of such men is that *they can suppress truth.* The positive advocacy which they go in for has much less affect; there effective falsehoods are much more falsehoods of silence than of active untruth, and mere boycott or silence can usually be pierced.

There have been a number of instances, as we all know, of a partial monopoly of information breaking down. Your own presidential elections in the United States are a very good example of that and so are many movements on our side. To have nearly the whole of the press against one will not necessarily mean that one will fail. But the boycott is another thing. When the few who control the mass of the press over a given large area agree to say nothing about some important matter, it is very difficult indeed to get that matter ventilated. We had a comic example of that over here in England two years ago. The whole available strength of our fleet was sent to the Mediterranean to frighten Italy. Hardly anyone in England heard of that because our press consented to be silent, but all over The rest of the world everybody heard of it, including, of course, the Italians, the only people from whom it was desired to keep it secret.

There is yet another force counter-balancing the monopolists of the press; this is what I have myself called in many an article and pamphlet the "free press." A little free weekly journal with quite small circulation will often have The power to break down a most formidable ring of silence or falsehood and there is also private conversation, passing on this efficient information received by the few who read the "free press." Such information spreads out in circles.

We had a very fine example of that half a lifetime ago in one of our innumerable political scandals, called the Marconi scandal. A little newspaper, with a circulation of not more than about 3,000 a week, run by Mr. G. Chesterton and myself did the whole work of the exposure in the face of complete boycott and silence by all the official press in England. It is true that culprits were not brought to justice. They continued to hold high office and to draw large fortunes out of the taxes, but at any rate they did not save their reputations.

There remains the freedom of the press in the matter of books and the better instructed magazines. This, as yet, is secure even over here, and on our side of the Atlantic, of course, it is still more secure. It is not secure under the despotisms; but wherever normal conditions of civic freedom exist the book is free. Now the effect of the book is very great. It has not the immediate effect of the monopolist daily press. The effect of the book is at long range. But it tells at last. If you want an example of that look at the effect of a book published eighty years ago, which at first hardly anybody read — the book called *Capital* by Karl Marx. It took a lifetime to produce its effect, but at the end of that lifetime it had given birth to international communism.

It may be asked what other remedy we have against the monopoly of information as it is now exercised through the more widely distributed newspapers. Well, we have or rather should have if we carry out our proper reforms, the remedy of public demand. A public possessed of well-distributed property will create a demand for information such as free citizens need and insist upon.

Most of the harm that is done by the monopolists of the modern popular press is only done because they appeal to men dependent upon wages, and enslaved by the industrial system. In their lack of security and their lack of sufficient freedom they develop an appetite for sensation. They are the less interested in civic business because they are not as much true citizens as their fathers were. For man is not a full citizen unless he is free; and a man is not fully free unless he has economic freedom. And economic freedom you cannot have without property, either individual or family or guild.

Chapter Twelve

Monopoly of Credit

How Bankers Creating and Controlling the "Promises Men Live By" Are Masters Over the Freedom of All Men in Debt.

Of all the forms of monopoly, the most dangerous today and the most powerful is the monopoly of Credit.

Here again, as in all other cases, the word "monopoly" must be rightly understood. Save in England, there is no complete monopoly of credit. In England the whole of the banking system, centered upon and gathering round the Bank of England, is one solid block. There is virtually no competition save the competition for customers between various branches of the great banks. The general banking policy is everywhere united.

In other countries banking is much more free, with the consequence that the clients of the banks are less secure. The credit system in England is the most stable in the world, because it is the most completely monopolized. The Bank of England and its dependents, the "Big Five" joint stock banks, have the most rapid and efficient banking methods in the world, and the security of their clients is almost absolute. But in other countries, such as France and the United States, (especially the United States before the crisis of 1929-31), having greater freedom of competition between various banking interests, depositors have also less security. Nevertheless, even with these, the power of the credit monopoly is very great. It is that form of money power which has the greatest strength in the modern world.

We must understand what it is. What is this "credit" which people talk of continually and take for granted, and yet is so rarely defined and which so very few people think clearly upon?

To answer that question, consider how the thing arose. In primitive conditions, credit, in the modern sense, was unknown.

Supposing of two neighbors one owned a pasture farm and one a tillage farm. Each could exchange his surplus produce against the surplus produce of the other. When multiple exchange rose up, that is, when not two units are involved but a number of units, the thing becomes more complicated; you cannot work the exchanges without a currency. The man with wheat says to the man with sheep, "I want timber." The man with sheep exchanges them for timber and then *may* exchange the timber with the wheat man. But very soon as more units are engaged they must have a common medium of exchange, or transactions could not be carried on. When, in the course of exchanges, a man is prepared to wait for payment, and so make the exchanges easier, that is the beginning of credit.

But credit has come to mean something very different today, because, *instead of currency being used for exchange, promises to pay are used for exchange,* and the banker who can get these promises to pay into circulation has practically created currency.

It began with goldsmiths and others receiving money of their neighbors for safe custody, giving a receipt for it, and prepared to give it back on demand. Then they found that only a certain proportion of the values they held were called for at any one time, and they took to lending out the balance at interest. Ten men had each put a thousand gold pieces into a neighbors custody for safe keeping. One and then another would draw out part of his treasure and later pay in new money. The man who was keeping the money and was acting as banker, found that at any one moment he was safe if he kept, say, one-tenth of the deposited money by him to meet claims as they came in, the other nine-tenths he could lend out at interest. That was the first step.

The second step was the banker "honoring checks." Originally that meant admitting that the man who had drawn the check had so much money at the bank, and had a right to have it paid him back on demand. But it soon came to mean something very different. The bankers, "extended a credit" to a customer. He said to a client, "You have not got a million at my bank, but you have premises and a business worth two million. If you want to build on to your factory mill I will, on your security, honor your checks up to half a million, but you must pay me interest for that credit."

Meanwhile he does the same thing with the builder, the farmer, the transport man and every other kind of client until at last the whole community are exchanging "instruments of credit," that is, the bankers' promises to pay instead of actual money, *and it lies entirely with the banker as to how much credit he shall advance and to whom.* In other words it lies entirely with the banker to decide whether human industry and such a direction shall, or shall not, proceed. By extending credits he can develop a property, or by reducing them leave it derelict.

The progress was not fully developed even one hundred years ago. Today it is universal and all powerful. So true it is that even nations fighting for their lives have got to go to the bankers for "credits" before they can get the weapons with which the state is to be defended.

This system of making currency "out of nothing," of making paper instruments of credit, virtually controls the modern world. The monopoly of credit, falling progressively into fewer and fewer hands, holds the lever upon which we all depend, and the monopolists of credit are the real masters of the state. This is, on the surface, only a political evil, and it is remote from the ordinary man. The ordinary man, living on a wage, may feel that he is being exploited by the capitalist with whom he deals. He has no way of seeing or feeling that the whole of society is also being exploited far more thoroughly by the controllers of credit, who draw tribute from all men and who can open or close the throttle of industrial energy at will.

This monopoly of credit only touches the ordinary man when he has a mortgage from a bank himself. The proletariat, living on a wage, is not aware of the new power. Yet it is the power which, more than any other, is threatening our civilization with ruin. For not only is it the master of all our activities, without our consent, but it is especially hard upon the small man and destructive of small ownership.

Today you may say that all society is in debt to those who hold the levers of credit, and that when, or if, we lose our freedom altogether we shall have for masters the remaining controllers of land and machinery, who will have behind them, as ultimate masters, the controllers of credit.

Chapter Thirteen

The End Is Slavery

The White Races of the World are Only Twenty Lifetimes Out of Slavery. The Christian Church Was the Influence Which Slowly Over the Centuries, Freed Man from His Serfdom. With the Decline of Religion the Tide Is Running the Other Way.

The *immediate* argument for reform is the inhuman condition to which industrial capitalism has reduced mankind wherever it has power: insufficiency of livelihood; insecurity; tyrannical routine; the absence of human conditions — the loss of "daily bread." These are the evils which cry out so insistently for remedy that men are in rebellion wherever such conditions exist. Therefore, I say, the *immediate* demand is for a reform that will get rid of these evils at once.

But those who see far enough ahead discover another ultimate reason for reform, perhaps more powerful than the immediate reason of today's injustice and intolerable circumstances. That *ultimate* motive is the dread of approaching slavery.

Things are going so fast that *if we do not take care slavery will return as a permanent institution among us.*

Put thus bluntly it sounds fantastic, but if you will look closely into the matter you will see how much there is to be said for those who warn us of that peril.

Remember that we, the white races, came only twenty lifetimes ago out of a state of society in which most men were slaves. A minority only were free men and masters. the others, who did the work, were chattels who worked for the advantage of those masters. For instance, in Britain at the time of St. Wilfrid, say AD 700, two families out of three were slaves: only one out of three was free.

That was a state of affairs taken for granted in all the pagan world. The slave was bought and sold, could be beaten, tortured or killed at the will of his owner.

Slavery was eliminated very slowly, only after generations of gradual change of heart, and the agent which got rid of it was the Christian Church.

As long as the old world was pagan, slavery was taken as a matter of course; but after the old world had been gradually converted, slavery began to disappear. First of all it became softened into serfdom, that is, a condition in which most men had to work for the minority of free men, but with *some* property and more freedom than of old. The serfs could not be personally bought and sold. The amount of work they had to perform for their masters was limited by custom and left them a certain margin of ownership in the soil they tilled or the instruments of the craft they pursued. Then from about AD 1000 to 1250, the serf became a free peasant and the craftsman became a free member of a craft guild.

With the gradual loss of religion, after AD 1500, the tide turned back again. Imperceptibly conditions which would ultimately favor a return to slavery appeared. With unrestricted competition men lost their holdings and the big landowner began to swallow up the independent farmer. In many places, notably in England after the Reformation, the local lord of the village began to absorb those farmers who had become free. the more fortunate farmers turned into a class of tenants, paying rents. The less fortunate became agricultural laborers at a wage that barely sufficed to keep them alive and working for the owners.

Later, the same process began to apply to the craftsmen. The old-fashioned tools were superseded by newer and more expensive instruments and the concentration of capital eliminated the smaller man. The smith, the carpenter, the independent small builder, all began to turn into people compelled to exist on a wage paid them by larger and larger concentrations of capital, controlled by fewer and fewer men.

The traditions of freedom remained for a long time. A man working at a wage was regarded by the law (he is still so regarded), as a free citizen: the equal of the man who employs him. But as the mass of men became destitute through the action of competition their power to contract freely disappeared. *There is no true contract between the man without anything and the man with capital behind him.* When the monopolies arose and gradually spread themselves over the social field, the insecurity and dependence of the wage-earner grew with them.

In order to preserve social peace there was instituted the device of "social relief." It is called by all sorts of names "assistance," "the dole" (that is the English name), "collective bargaining" (with the collective contracts guaranteed by the state) and all the rest of it — but the true name of this new series of arrangements for making capitalism work is "state socialism."

Men out of work are provided with the bare necessities of life by the state; but to make that system function it is necessary that there should be inquisition into a man's condition, and when he is offered work he may be forced to take it. Regulations were made to maintain minimum rates of wage but nothing was done to restore property and without property he can have no true economic freedom. The worker, with greater security and fuller sufficiency than he had had before, remained as much a wage-slave as ever. Indeed, he was more of a wage-slave than before because a whole organization was growing up which supervised his activities, ordered his life, and saw to it that he worked for the advantage of others, the owners of those means of production which the worker himself did not possess.

Now when such a state of affairs takes root, when a generation shall have grown up which takes that state of affairs for granted, men will equally take for granted the social fact that they eat and are clothed and live and work under the power of others. If you were to take away the control of capital from the possessing class, and vest in the officers of the community all the land and the housing and the stores of food and clothing and machinery, etc. the individual citizen would still be at the mercy of the officials of the state. In the long run that would inevitably turn into his being at the mercy of a caste of officials. the man who is now a citizen would be first run, then owned by a small body of his fellow men.

When all these palliatives for our economic evils have been applied, they will, if we continue on the present lines, have reestablished what will be in practice *slavery*.

A man may say, "Well! I am pretty well a slave now, anyhow! It is better to be a slave guaranteed in his livelihood than a slave hopelessly insecure and perhaps underfed, ill-housed and under-clothed." By all means: but do not forget that while this public payment you accept makes the coming of slavery more comfortable it does not dispel the moral fact of slavery.

A man is now compelled to work for another man indirectly through a supposed "free contract." If you destroy the system whereby he can make that contract and can be bound to it, the only ultimate alternative — save property — is a legal position in which he is *compelled* to work for the state. He may comfort himself with the thought that all his fellow citizens are also compelled to work for the state. That does not make him any less a slave: and if he admits slavery to the state he will end at last in slavery to a class of officials who will become a master-class.

There are only two alternatives; the restoration of property to a number of families sufficient to give their tone to the whole state, or a drift towards slavery.

Property is the guarantee of economic freedom, and the only guarantee.

But before asking ourselves how property may be restored to the mass of men under modern conditions, we will examine the other remedies proposed and see in what they fail.

Chapter Fourteen

The Way Out

*In the First Thirteen Articles of This Series Mr.
Belloc Has Discussed the Intolerable Social Evils
Which Industrial Capitalism Has Brought About.
He Now Turns to the Remedies: True and False.*

There are four main proposals offered for setting things
right again, and finding our way out of the dreadful state
into which we have fallen. The first three are false remedies,
the fourth is the true remedy, which is the restoration of
property, the building up of economic freedom for the mass
of men, and the re-creating of that independence of the
family which industrial capitalism has destroyed. Much the
greater part of this series will deal in detail with this true
remedy, the restoration of property; but first of all we must
examine the false remedies. It is urgent that we should examine them because they are clamoring to be put into practice,
and the worse and the more false they are, the greater is their
attraction.

These three remedies are, in the order of their falsehood and their imperfection, first, communism, which is the worst; secondly the guaranteeing of capitalism by the state; and thirdly, that most interesting and well known but illusory scheme called National Credit. I am going to deal with each of these in turn before talking of how to reach the true remedy of property, coupled with a guild system and with state control of monopolies.

Communism makes a violent and direct appeal because it is "radical," in the original sense of the word "radical," which means, "going to the root." Communism goes to the root of the matter. It proposes to get rid at one blow of all the evils from which the modern industrialized proletariat suffers. The man for whom the pressure of those conditions has made life intolerable, grasps at the communist remedy as a man dying of thirst would grasp a pitcher of clear-looking water — not knowing that it was poisoned. The appeal of communism is so immediate, so plain, so comprehensible to every intelligence and so complete that, wherever industrial capitalism exists, men flock to it. The idea arouses enthusiasm in the oppressed and men are prepared to devote themselves to it as to a new religion.

We shall see in a moment why, in spite of these advantages, communism is not only to be condemned in plain morals and common sense, but also why it is on the way to partial failure already.

The second false remedy — State-guaranteed capitalism — is of high importance because it is being more and more applied in England, England being the country which first gave birth to industrial capitalism, the country whose language covers so great a part of the earth and the country which lends itself more than any other to successful political experiment. This false remedy has also taken root in England because it is the country in which, more than any other, men are prepared to obey laws in the making of which they have had little or no part.

It is not easy to find a name for this second false remedy, for, although it is already in full swing on our side of the Atlantic, it has not been given an official title; but we must give it a name if we are to deal with it at all: let us call it "secure capitalism." It is not state socialism (as it is often called), though it is accompanied by many features of state socialism. The characteristic of this second false remedy, both in motive and in plan, is the saving of capitalism by certain reforms which, it is hoped, will make it stable and permanent; the most important of these reforms being the maintenance of the unemployed proletariat out of the taxes.

The obvious evils of modern industrial capitalism, the evils which come home to all its victims and that are most acutely felt, are insecurity and insufficiency. Industrial capitalism, being defined as a condition in which wealth is produced by instruments the direction of which is vested in a wealthy minority and *not* in the workers who use those instruments, there follows all that set of evils which we have been describing and announcing in these articles. Of these evils, I repeat, the quite obvious ones, which millions have

experienced and violently resent, are insufficiency of livelihood and the insecurity even of that insufficient livelihood.
It is difficult to say which of these two evils is the more desperate, each of them as driven masses of men to the verge
of revolution, and the two combined were rendering life impossible in the industrialized countries.

Now "secure" or "State-guaranteed" capitalism is a system wherein these two immediate and obvious evils disappear. Insecurity disappears because the livelihood of every
citizen is guaranteed by the state at a certain fixed rate. We
find, when the system is complete (as it is already nearly
complete in Great Britain), that the only difference between
the employed and the unemployed man is that the employed
man *may* have (he does not always have) more to subsist on
than the unemployed man. Insufficiency also disappears, in
theory at least, for the public assistance given to the families
that cannot obtain wages is calculated on a certain minimum, supposed to be sufficient to keep men clothed and fed
and housed.

But "secure" or "State-guaranteed" capitalism, capitalism in its new reformed state, continues to manifest the original spiritual evil connected with all capitalism, which evil is
the misuse of property; the special power of a small class of
citizens, strong through no agency but their wealth, and the
exploitation of the mass of men by masters to whom they
owe no loyalty and with whom they have no spiritual tie.

When we come to study this proposed remedy of "guaranteed capitalism" in detail we shall see to what final evils

this major spiritual evil of capitalism leads, however secure the livelihood of the people under it.

The third false remedy is the least bad and also the most interesting. It is the remedy called "National Credit." It is associated with the name of its brilliant original expositor, who may well be called its discoverer, Major Douglas, and is therefore often called "the Douglas Scheme of National Credit." The central idea of this reform is to check up the total productive power of the community and then distribute to all members of the community credit tickets which will provide them with purchasing power equivalent to the total possible production. Supposing that in a community there are stores of raw material and plant capable of producing a hundred billion dollars worth of goods, and that the community is only actually producing fifty billion dollars' worth, there is a margin of another fifty billions which is not in existence, but which could be called into existence by citizens presenting their credit tickets as payment for the goods they desire. How it is proposed to make the scheme work we shall see later when we come to consider it in detail. It is enough to say for the moment that it has the great advantage over the other two that it neither exploits men nor degrades them. There is nothing servile about it. The man with his credit ticket at the end of the week, giving him purchasing power over and above his regular wages, sufficient to buy, say, a good overcoat, makes his choice of the article as freely as the richest man buying the same under our present conditions. The wage-earner will live (according to the supporters of the National Credit Scheme) in the same sort of way he did before, but only with this difference: that he will have a much more satisfactory income through having a larger and a regular purchasing power. As we shall see, when we come to the details of this scheme a few articles ahead, there is a great deal to be said against it., and that is why I have called it a false remedy; but it is not false in the sense that it is bad morals or inhuman. It does not rob anyone; it does not in theory oppress anyone. It does not even order anyone about.

Here, then, we have the three main remedies proposed: 1. communism; secure, or guaranteed, capitalism; 3. national credit. Now let us go into each of these in turn and see why we have called them false remedies.

Chapter Fifteen

Communism: The Theory

Communism, like every other political system, has two aspects: the Abstract and the Concrete. It is based on a theory, an idea; and also it has in real life a certain way of going on, habits and practices, which do not seem at first sight to be necessarily connected with that idea, but which *are* found appearing in connection with it. In this first article we will go into the idea of communism and see why it is a false remedy. In the next we will go into the practice and see how abominable in practice communism becomes.

The economic idea of communism in itself, that is, the mere plan or pattern, seems at first sight neither good nor evil, any more than a mathematical proposition is good or evil. You can state communism in this fashion so that it is apparently quite free from any moral taint, and appears as a system which anyone is free to accept or to let alone, according to his inclination. Stated thus, theoretically, the principle of communism is simply this: that public authority shall not protect the property of any man when that property is used for production, distribution or exchange. Communism proposes that there shall be no right of property in land or houses or ships or stores of food or machinery of any kind, when those things are used for producing further wealth, because this leads to poor men working for the advantage of rich men.

Communism has no objection to a man consuming wealth on a large scale, even luxuriously. If you can earn a large income as a singer, for instance, the communist state is quite agreeable that you should spend it on anything you like for your own pleasure. But you must not invest any of it. For when you invest you are creating a capitalist function. If you invest in railway shares, for instance, you do so in order to get an income without working for it: an income which is produced by the labor of some other man. In the same way, and for the same reasons, communism forbids inheritance. You may spend what you earn, you may even spend it luxuriously, but you must not accumulate it and leave it to your children, lest they should use it for the capitalist exploitation of their fellows.

If I have a fine schooner which my sons and I can sail together, communism makes no objection to our doing so as an amusement; but it forbids us to use that vessel for carrying goods or for any other useful purpose associated with profit.

Stated thus, the moral argument in favor of communism seems a strong one. The exploitation of one man by another is not a moral act, nor the forbidding of it, apparently, an immoral act. Moreover, thousands of good men and great numbers of actual saints have lived under purely communistic conditions, for those are the conditions of most religious orders. The community owns everything, the individual owns nothing, save what he actually consumes, and this ownership of all by the community is (apparently) communism.

So far, so good. And communism thus stated as an ideal, appeals to the generous and the simple. Where, then, is the snag in the mere theory of communism? The defender of communism will say, "No doubt such and such a group of communists did behave very badly, but that has nothing to do with the communist theory. The violence and the outrages and the rest of it are not logically connected with this simple conception of common ownership of all the means of production, distribution and exchange."

There is another cogent argument in favor of communism which we often hear used, and which seems at first sight irrefutable. It is this: when we are actually using, as a community, goods belonging to the community, when we are therefore acting in the communist fashion, no suffering results but rather good. In Switzerland (Switzerland is the freest and perhaps the happiest of all democracies), where the railroads are owned by the community, no one using the railroads feels any different from men using the railroads which belong to capitalist organizations in England or the United States. When you enjoy the amenities of a public park you are enjoying communal property. So your communist can say again, "Where is the snag?" expecting the answer "There is none."

Everything about communism, in theory at least, seems good, and it manifestly gets rid of a lot of evils which accompany private property. But the man who says, "Where is the snag?" and expects the answer "There is none" is shortsighted. There is a serious and obvious snag indeed, which is this: that though the public ownership of this or of that creates no injustice and does no violence to human nature, the public ownership of *everything,* the forbidding of the private citizen and his family to own land or house or plough or cattle, means that *whoever owns those things — that is, the state — is the absolute master of the dispossessed communist citizen.* Why that is the very argument the communists themselves have used (just as anybody else has, who has thought at all about the industrial problem) when they condemn capitalism! "The capitalist class," says the communist, "by retaining in its power the land and the instruments of production, is the master of the mass of citizens who do not own those things." Exactly! And the same is ten times truer of universal public ownership. The state (which means, in practice, the Officials) is as much the master of the communist masses as a slave driver is of his slaves. He may wish the slaves well or he may wish them ill. That has nothing to do with the system. He may be generous or he may be cruel. His absolute power has nothing to do with that. communism, even as a theory, denies the most elementary right of mankind: the right of choice, the right of ordering one's own life.

It is no reply to this major accusation (which of itself damns the whole system irremediably) to say that present conditions are intolerably bad. No doubt they are; but one must not fly to a remedy worse than the disease. There is, indeed, one type of man who apologizes for communism, rather reluctantly, something like this: "No doubt communism is a bad thing, but it is the only chance we have, for, under the effect of modern machinery, monopoly is inevitable. When monopoly is inevitable it is better to vest it in the state than in a few individuals."

When such a reply is made we touch on the very heart of communism. We see its nature plainly exposed. It is the fruit of capitalist mentality. It is an evil remedy bred of an evil thing. Industrial capitalism talks in exactly this way of "inevitably monopoly" which is not inevitable at all. Under communism we should have all the worst spiritual effects of industrial capitalism extended and emphasized because their tyranny would be universal. It would be the killing of the soul of man and its dignity. Now it is precisely because of this character in it that communism only comes into being under conditions of horror. It is because the thing is theoretically inhuman that its fruits are the fruits of inhumanity, appalling cruelty and an appalling contempt for human life. It is a most superficial, false, analysis which can see no connection between communist theory and the abominations which accompany communism in action. When you destroy the family and the sanctity of the individual, when you make war on the tradition of human culture, you are making war on the Image of God. And because you are making war on the Image of God, which is Man, with his human dignity and free will, you find yourself at once at war with God Himself. It is not an accident that communism should produce wholesale massacre, arson, torture, and the destruction of all lovely things. A perverse theory produces perverse acts. The story has been told over and over again but it can never be told too often. In my next article I will describe those main experiences of communism and show what this Anti-Christ essentially is, getting his driving power from hate and feeding his detestable life on human souls.

Chapter Sixteen

Communism Is Wicked!

Everywhere Communism Begins with Massacre and
Continues with Murder Because Only by Terror Can Men
Be Forced to Support a Remedy That Is Against the Spirit.

Communism is a false remedy to the evils which capitalism has brought upon us. We have seen that it is a false remedy; but there are two other things about it all important for us to understand. The first is that it is evil, not a mere economic theory to be tested like a mathematical or an engineering theory, but a moral theory and a wicked one. The second is that those who rely upon communism as a remedy will be in a worse case than if they had not tried any remedy at all, for communism must necessarily break down, but not till it has done vast harm.

I will deal with the first of these points today, and with the second in my next article.

How can one say that communism is morally evil, not as a theory but as a thing? There is nothing morally evil in a number of men getting together and agreeing to hold all they have in common. But the specific remedy for modern capitalism, called "communism," is wicked in its action because *it is evil in its motive and driving power*. With many men when they first turn to communism the motive is quite different from the motives of those who started and who still, with increasing difficulty, maintain the communist effort against society. The motive of the first converts, and of the newly made converts every day, is partly indignation against the horrible social injustices of our time (an indignation which is often felt even more strongly by those who look on than by those who actually suffer). It is partly made up of the appeal to simplicity, for it is the most obvious and easiest and quickest way out of the complicated tangle of injustice into which society has fallen. But behind the whole thing is something different from excusable motives of this kind. Behind the whole thing is hatred of human traditions, chief of which is the tradition of worship of God, and of revealed morals and natural religion, which are the best inheritance of mankind.

If proof were needed of the essential wickedness of the movement and of the falsehood of pretending that it is a mere effort at redressing existing wrongs, we have but to consider how communism has acted in practice and before our eyes. If it had been what it pretends to be, it would have begun by a straightforward pronouncement of its aims, purely economic and social. It would have proceeded to apply the new laws with as much respect for humanity and decency as possible. It would have worked as all great human reforms work, mainly by persuasion. It would have excited loyalty and affection. That is the order in which the thing would have developed if it were what it pretends to be.

Now we all know that the actual order in which it developed was quite different. It began, wherever it broke out, with indiscriminate massacre. It did not merely murder the rich — that would have been bad enough — a mere act of blood and revenge. It did not even begin by examining cases to hand and withdrawing economic control from capitalist organizations. It began with blind murder, and murder on such a scale as humanity had never known before. The only distant parallel to the horror was the invasion of the savage Mongols, in the thirteenth century, inspired by a similar hatred of all that was civilized and traditional in human society, when they turned the wealth of Mesopotamia into the howling desert it has remained ever since.

Communism, I say, began with massacre! That must be carefully remembered. *It began with massacre.* Massacre was not an unfortunate outburst, the result of its establishment; it was the preliminary and most heartfelt spontaneous expression of its spirit. It *began* with massacre in Russia, in Hungary, and quite recently in Spain.

The second point is this: the massacre was not primarily nor mainly a massacre of those who exploited the proletariat. It was mainly, as a beginning, a massacre of men and women devoted to religion, and a destruction of shrines devoted to religion. That has been the brand characteristic hallmark of the thing. Everybody noted it at once in Russia, but Russia was a long way off, and the picture was confused. The other day in Spain the picture was clear-cut and vivid. All Europe woke up to what had happened. The wild beast was primarily concerned with destroying the ministers of the Christian Faith, and the men and women devoted to religion, and the burning and looting of churches. The one thing that damned you and threatened your life in the communist rising was not an appearance of wealth, though that often was dangerous; the one thing fatal was a religious element in the victims.

But communism did not only begin everywhere with massacre, it does not only begin everywhere by drawing up a list of victims to be murdered wholesale and without trial, it *continues* the habit; it lives by terror and by mass-killing. The whole method of the government in communist Russia has been of that sort, and the whole method of government in communist Spain has been of that sort. It everywhere reposes upon terror: the terror of blind violence.

If it be asked why such an atmosphere of incredible evil surrounds the thing, seeing that there is no apparent logical connection between the communist theory and vast indiscriminate bloodshed, torture, burning and the rest, the answer is not difficult to find. There is a connection. The connection is this: that communism proposes an imposition by force of something repulsive to the spirit of man. *You cannot get men to accept an order which is against nature and against every good human instinct, save by the inhuman and abnormal method of continuous terror.*

COMMUNISM IS WICKED!

I have talked to not a few men who had been attracted towards communism in the first instance by a sense of justice, combined with a desire for the simplification of things: the untying of the tangled knot into which capitalism had got our affairs. In all but very few cases I have found in these men varying degrees of disgust with the savor of the air with which they had mixed. Some felt it more strongly than others. Many felt it so strongly that they ended by a hatred of that which they had been led to believe was a solution of their ills. Some, indeed, only felt a general revulsion and continued to make dwindling excuses. All who came in from genuine compassion, or from a genuine desire for a better order, have manifested disappointment, leading to disgust, from experiencing the thing itself — all save one small minority.

For I have indeed found among such men as had been led in at first from good motives a small minority who were, so far as one can say it of men still alive — damned. That is, they had suffered a perversion of the will. They had got into a state of mind in which the wreaking of hatred against their fellow beings was a greater pleasure to them than the establishment of what they had once thought was justice. They were perverted. They had been turned into the likeness of the criminals who introduced this foul thing into our midst. But for the rest I found everywhere in varying degrees a growing reaction against what, in the beginning, they had hoped would be a "way out," a remedy, the solution of the problem of capitalism.

To take up a remedy for a disease, which remedy is worse than the disease itself, is mere folly. To settle your anger at an injustice by committing a murder is a moral insanity. To fly to communism as a cure for capitalism is an action of that kind.

But it is something more. It is a folly in practice as well as in morals. The remedy is not only worse than the disease, but is a remedy which cannot but fail and is, indeed, already failing. This is a capital, practical point which will more and more appeal to everyone, even to that large number who do not believe, being rational beings, in the all importance of morals.

Communism is failing, and must fail. Those who expect relief by way of communism will be left high and dry. They will not get the imaginary good which they may have expected. They will find only failure, and how and why this should be so I will describe in my next article.

Chapter Seventeen

Communism Has Failed

*Even In Russia the Intelligent Observer Can Detect
the Trend Toward the Normal Human Tradition,
While Other Nations Are in Violent Revolt Against It.*

In every place that communism has been tried, not only has
it in part failed, but it is in process of further failing.

The distinction between the breakdown, and the contin-
uance of breakdown, is important. The one is static, the
other is dynamic. A mere example of breakdown here and
there, even the repetition of it, is not sufficient to prove that
the thing which has broken down is, in its nature, unworkable.
The breakdowns may be due to particular circumstances
which can be looked into and set right. After a certain number of breakdowns their frequency may lessen.

But if the breakdown of any system or theory becomes
both continuous and increasing, if you get more and more
examples of breakdown and less evidence of recovery from
breakdown, then we may definitely say that the thing has

been tested and is failing, though the failing may not yet have reached the last limit of failure. A man gets into a queer way financially long before he goes bankrupt. A man usually suffers from illness before he dies. So, when you follow the curve of development and see any experiment or theory working out worse and worse, you may say that the thing attempted, even before it completely fails, is of the nature of failure.

It is like taking the wrong trail across the mountains by night. The further you go the more unfamiliar the path gets, and the more unfamiliar your surroundings become. After a certain time you are half-persuaded that you have taken a wrong turning; you are fairly certain of it before the daybreak shows you that you have reached a place quite different from that for which you were heading.

The first evidence of the breakdown of communism after its emergence from the theoretical stage and its inception as an active force in practice, was the vigorous reaction of sane and normal men against it. That was what happened in Hungary and that was what happened in Bavaria. It did not happen in Russia at once in the mass of the people because Russia was almost entirely, in its social life, a country of peasants who had always lived on their own farms or on land which they held more or less in a communal life with their neighbors. The communist breakdown came to them as a piece of distant news: all that they knew in practice was that they would apparently have more land, or possession of land less burdened. They did not know that they were threatened with inhuman conditions. When they did find out what communism meant, The risings began — and they have continued ever since. They have not been universal, still less have they been universally successful; but they have been successive and have continued. They have been provoked by famine, by arbitrary seizure of the peasants' produce, and by the whole inhuman theory imposed by communism on the state.

In Spain the reaction came a few weeks after society had been stunned by the first outrages. When it came it was vigorous and had the main living force of the nation behind it. It is true that the victims of capitalism, the industrial proletariat, who had directly suffered from such measure of industrial capitalism as had existed in Russia or in Spain, did not join in the reaction against the revolution attempted in the one case and achieved in the other. But taking society as a whole, Spain reacted. It is also most significant that that part of Spain, the organized proletariat of the industrial centers, of the mines of the northwest, of the greater industrialized cities — notably Barcelona — did not adopt communism. Their leaning was towards anarchy for perhaps most of them, but for a very large section a guild system, the ownership of machinery and instruments of production by corporations.

Communism, as communism, failed, and has continued to fail even in that eastern part of Spanish territory which is still officially "Red." I have heard at first hand the inward conviction that communism must fail, as witnessed to from within as well as from without. I am personally informed at first hand of a conversation most significant in this regard. The head of a very great state indeed related to me a colloquy held between him and the communist statesman — if the word "statesman" can be used — who is perhaps the best known of the bunch. The head of the state treated this strange visitor courteously, and asked him, as one responsible observer to another, what he thought of the fortunes of the new thing, that new thing which we are all growing to detest more and more as its practice develops. The communist leader said to him, "At the beginning whatever we were in theory we were, in power and actual practice, zero. We rose rapidly in effective power. In one great country, Russia, we seized all the levers of authority; we seized them partially elsewhere. Now we have got about halfway, but at a slackening pace." He added that it must be so with all revolutionary movements, that they would come to a maximum and then begin to find difficulties.

That was his confession. He did not, he could not, speak out what was presumably in his mind — his sense that the thing had failed.

This man had started out with a certain conviction: that the capitalist world being what it was, with an inflamed and angry proletariat ready to rise, communism would sweep the board. A few years of experience had begun to teach him wisdom. He was beginning to say "fifty-fifty." In a few years more he will put the chances lower than that. For in truth communism has failed. Even where it has gathered votes, as in modern France, its effect is limited to the industrial areas and the votes do not express so much a positive desire for communist revolution as a natural hatred of capital injustice.

No doubt to many of my readers the phrase "communism has failed" will seem an exaggeration. Probably *in the near future* the phrase will seem more false than it does to those who are reading it here on this page today. Nevertheless that phrase is true. Though the communist vote shall increase (and it probably will somewhat increase in the industrial areas of Europe *in the near future*); though the repression of communism in other areas has to rely upon abnormal methods, yet it is true to say that communism is on the downgrade. The tide is falling, and those who have depended upon the exceptional upheaval will find themselves high and dry. Not that remedy; some other more permanent human and normal remedy must be sought; for those who trust to the remedy of communism will discover that not only the plain morals of mankind, the undying conscience of mankind, but the mere material circumstances, the world that surrounds them, are incompatible with communism in action.

There is one other piece of evidence, not easily appreciated by those who live far off from Europe, nor even too easily appreciated by those who live in the west of Europe. Communism has had to be modified, wherever it has won an initial victory. It has had to be modified particularly in Russia, wherein it rose with such devastating fury, where it proclaimed itself to be, and was thought to be, by every observer, triumphant. The whole state, the arrangement of society, the tilling and management of the land, is slowly and gradually, but continuously, reverting towards normal human tradition.

The reaction is very far from complete, but all those who visit agricultural Russia return with the same story: the re-establishment of man in his normal function of a tiller of the soil, enjoying the fruits of his own labor, continuing the family and, by his tillage, supporting his immediate posterity, is already apparent. It is only a beginning. Russian society will have a long way to go before the vast inhuman evil of twenty years ago is replaced by something sane and livable. There is as yet no official recognition in Russia of the continuous family, no right of inheritance, no fully admitted and legal guaranteed possession by the small man of his freedom and of that property without which freedom is impossible. But the stream is going that way increasingly, and those rare outsiders who watch what is proceeding in the very homeland of communism bear witness to the direction of that stream.

Chapter Eighteen

Property

The way out is to re-establish property; destitution means nothing else than the absence of property. We say of the destitute man that he is *compelled* to obey a master, because property in the means of livelihood are in that master's hands. To be paid a sufficient wage is not the same thing as to own; for he who pays the wage controls him who receives it.

The whole meaning of property is the economic freedom which it bestows upon the individual or family possessing it. Well-distributed property does not create special privilege, it does not enable men to live without working and to exploit the labor of others while they themselves are idle. A man who lives in his own house exploits no one. A man possessing his share in the factory in which he works exploits no one. A man possessing national bonds, the proceeds of which are equivalent to the taxes he pays for the meeting of the interest of national bonds, exploits no one. The interest he receives will not be exactly equivalent to his share of taxpaying to meet such interest. Some will have more, some less. But a widely distributed national debt creates no sense of social injustice. It is the few taxing the many that does so. All the theoretical injustice of attaching to exploitation of one class by another lessens and nearly disappears where property is fully distributed. Where it is *only* income that is well distributed men are still under the thumb of whoever or whatever pays that income, but where ownership is well distributed the owners are, all of them, free men.

Of course, an exact distribution of ownership would be an ideal, and therefore impossible, state of affairs: but a condition of society in which the greater part of citizens owned enough to be economically free is practicable, and possible of attainment. So far from being an imaginary Utopian scheme it has been accepted for centuries throughout societies numbering millions and is to be found peaceably and successfully at work over the greater part of the civilized earth at this moment. Only where men are living under the curse of industrial capitalism is well-divided property unfamiliar.

Yes, a redistribution of property so that a sufficient proportion of citizens may own is the "Way Out," and the *only* human and just and permanent way out, from the crying evils of industrial capitalism and the servile conditions which it threatens to produce unless we apply our remedy in time.

Well-distributed property is its own guarantee of survival. It produces among the owners customs and laws — the guild and the village community — which prevent property from falling into the hands of the few. It builds up of itself the habits required for the preservation of economic freedom. You may see that for yourselves by watching society at work in any country where property is already well distributed.

Here it will be objected that well-distributed property is not possible in modern industry on account of the expense of the great new instruments of production. "the smith," we are told, "The carpenter at his bench, the cobbler and his handmade boots, have gone forever because centralized power and the new machinery which it activates has driven the small producer from the field. In the same way the large store and a chain of stores in the same hands, have driven the small distributor from the field. You may," it is admitted, "restore well divided property among independent farmers, but you can never, in future, restore it among industrial workers."

Now this argument is false in two ways. First, it is false because even the most expensive machinery can belong, and does belong, as we all know, to shareholders. Secondly, it is false because a great deal of that concentration of property which is called "inevitable" is not inevitable at all. It is merely the product of uncontrolled competition.

Discovery and invention have, it is true, produced much larger industrial units of production than our fathers knew — for instance in the way of ships, of land transport, and instruments and materials used for building. But discovery and invention also advantaged certain lesser units. There is no better example of this than the electric motor and the facile distribution of electric power. These between them could have restored masses of small producers had they been taken advantage of in time.

In other words, there is still plenty of room for the small units of industrial production. Where the nature of the new instruments makes small units impossible there is nothing to prevent those who work with the large new units holding those units co-operatively as members of a guild.

The *idea* of the guild has almost died out because the anarchy and greed of the modern world has destroyed the *thing*, but there is nothing to prevent its being restored.

The guild is essentially an association of free owners who work co-operatively any instrument which is too expensive for separate ownership by a single member. The great sculptures of the middle ages were produced by guilds using instruments quite beyond reach of the small individual members, but easily obtainable and controlled by the community of owners.

Let it be remembered that this aim of ours for the restoration of private property among a determining number of the community, the distribution of property among the masses of citizens who should thus be made free, does not contradict state ownership of certain functions. What it contradicts is the false doctrine of general or preponderant state ownership, or what is worst of all universal state ownership. The state exists for the family and the individual; not these for the state.

In many European countries where highly divided property is the rule, railways are state owned, and in all without exception, the Post Office. There is no hard and fast line, but the general principle is clear enough. Any free and well-ordered state includes a proportion of state ownership which is based upon private ownership in the hands of as many citizens and families as possible at any rate, of so many as to make the principle determining character of society. Such ownership may be co-operative in the form of the guild where large units are necessary or as in the case of nearly all agriculture and a great deal of industry as well, owned in small units by craftsmen.

The function of distribution should also follow the same lines. Where there *must* be concentration in a large unit, that unit should be organized as a guild; but in the vast majority of cases a small unit of distribution — the small store — is sufficient.

Chapter Nineteen

Secured Capitalism

*The Enslavement of Men to the State Under the Social Security
Palliatives in a Planned Economy Is as Bad as Communism.*

Industrial capitalism is the product of two things acting together: one good, one evil. The good thing is political freedom; the bad thing is destitution, that is lack of property in
the masses.

Political freedom pre-supposes that all citizens are equal
and free to choose and order their own lives. Therefore they
can only be bound to render services by contract. There is
no slavery. Destitution affecting the greater part of citizens
— that is, a state of society in which most citizens own nothing — leaves the mass of families at the mercy of the minority who own capital: that is, the food, clothing, housing,
etc. whereby alone man can live. The destitute man is legally
bound by his contract to the capitalist for whom he has
engaged to work for a wage. He is free not to work for such a
master; but it is only freedom to starve. Moreover, the

minority who own are under no compulsion to employ the majority who are destitute. There follow on this combination of freedom and destitution the very evil consequences of industrial capitalism, which have become intolerable and which threaten to upset all our civilization.

We saw that an obvious immediate remedy for such evils was communism; for communism proposed to get rid of insecurity and insufficiency — the intolerable conditions attaching to industrial capitalism. But it only does so at the expense of destroying freedom. It makes all men slaves to the officials of the state. It is inhuman and a remedy worse than the disease.

Now there is another remedy which has not only been suggested but put into practice, it has already taken deep root in Europe, particularly in the industrial parts of Europe, and especially in England. This other remedy may be called *"secured capitalism."* Its object is a society in which the existing minority of owners who now control the mass of destitute men shall continue to control them and make a profit out of their labor, *but to do so securely,* without fear of revolt from the destitute. The danger of such revolt lies in the insecurity of livelihood among all the destitute and the insufficient income of most of them. To remove these causes of unrest the destitute man is guaranteed subsistence by the state in sickness and a minimum pittance to support him in old age. At the same time the destitute citizen, the wage-earner without property and therefore without economic freedom, is securely bound to the capitalistic machine. He is listed, his movements are known and traced, he is controlled by the state for the benefit of the capitalist scheme.

This system is ushered in and sustained by a number of new institutions with which people are getting more and more familiar, "compulsory arbitration," "compulsory insurance against unemployment and sickness," "old age pensions," and so on. These are called in England by the general term "social services," and in them lies the greatest danger of the present moment, for they avoid sudden change, they fit in with existing capitalist society and they do not openly challenge freedom. But as they become fixed habits they *lead to the re-establishment of servitude*, and they are the more likely to reach that bad conclusion at last from the fact that their effect is veiled under phrases which conceal their ultimate action.

The wage-earner out of work is kept alive by state officials spending state money on him. They must keep complete control over him lest he should be taking advantage of the system. If he is earning a little money "on the side" this money must be counted against the minimum relief to which he is entitled. If he earns just enough to keep body and soul together he is entitled to no relief, and a close watch must be kept on his chance receipts to make certain that he has no claim on public money.

Again: in order to make the system work it is necessary to divide citizens into two classes: those who own or possess more than a certain weekly amount and those who earn less. This has already been done in England. To obtain payment during unemployment through compulsory insurance, he must carry a card telling the officials all about him and when and how he was employed, and at what rate. The same goes for his claim to sick benefit. So with old age pensions, a person over sixty-five, for instance, will be paid so much a week by state officials if he is *earning nothing on his own*. Whatever little he might earn as a free man, or might possess, is immediately counted against his pension. His affairs must, therefore, be under perpetual investigation and control.

If he saves anything the amount he has saved will count against any claim to relief. If he has saved enough to buy a little property, such as the house he lives in, the rental value of that house will count against him in the same way.

When the whole scheme is working fully and covering all the propertyless wage earners of a large industrial society, that society is completely controlled by officials whose activities make secure the capitalist system. When such a state of affairs has gone on for a lifetime and men have come to take it for granted, not only the incentive to accumulate small property but the possibility of doing so will have disappeared.

Moreover the power to refuse relief soon involves the power to dictate what work a man shall do. A man will have to take, on compulsion, any work offered him through the officials, or ordered by them.

The whole thing makes for slavery in the long run, as much as communism does. But whereas communism is

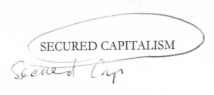

known for the evil thing it is and can be met by direct attack, arrangements for securing capitalism in this new fashion insinuate themselves gradually and establish themselves, as it were, by a trick. Secured capitalism such as we now have universally in England, and such as is being clamored for by many reformers all over the industrial world, is death to any hope of restoring property to the mass of families — without which restoration human dignity in general and economic freedom are impossible.

Here will be asked, "But are not such relief payments necessary under present conditions? We cannot allow men to starve. We must provide the destitute against sickness, unemployment and old age."

Yes: these various schemes are palliatives against intolerable immediate evils, *but they are only palliatives*. They are necessary because you are dealing with destitute men. When the masses own the instruments with which they work and the things that keep them alive such palliatives will not be necessary. For when we restore property and with it the independence of the family and of the individual, the chief evils of capitalism will have disappeared. But if we build up the state on such palliatives we destroy our chance of restoring property. They cease to be palliatives, they become inevitable universal social functions. They destroy freedom altogether and re-introduce servitude.

Use palliatives by all means; in fact you *must* use them unless you are to take refuge in communism; but get rid of them as soon as possible, and substitute for them well-divided property so that man shall be free. There are cases of physical failure where you must, perhaps, give a large dose of spirit to save a man's life, but make a habit of it and you will ruin him.

determining number

Chapter Twenty

Towards Reform

*Whenever a Determining Number of People Learn of
Their Exploitation by a Few Who Control Wealth in
Their Own Hands — When Enough People Care — We
Will Begin to Make Progress. Reforms Must Be Worked Out,
an Immediate Innovation of the Most Desired Reforms
Might Create Chaos Worse Than the Endured Abuses.*

There is a very important principle to be recognized in attempting any modern reform: it is the principle of the "Determining Number." In any society any particular institution
gives its tone to the whole of that society, not because it is
universal, not because it affects *every* citizen, but if it affects a
determining number of those citizens. For instance, we say that
the old pagan society of Greece and Rome, at the moment
when it was undergoing conversion by the Church, was a
slave society. The slaves were not, perhaps, the majority.
there was certainly at least a third of free men even in the
worst patches. Nevertheless slavery was the institution which

marked that society. Or again, we say of a Christian society that it is based on marriage. Not that every person is married. Counting the children, the celibates, the widows and widowers, there may even be a majority not married: but marriage is the basis of that society, taken for granted, and giving it its tone.

Now when attempting any great reform, such as the destruction of industrial capitalism and its replacement by a society of economically free men who own the materials with which they work, we can hardly expect to create a society in which every single family or individual should be thus an owner. We shall have achieved our end when a *determining number* of that society are economically free men, and therefore fit for political freedom. If we refuse to consider schemes which could not apply to the whole community, to every single individual, if we will only consider schemes which are universal and have no exceptions, two things are certain. First, we shall not succeed in establishing such a scheme; secondly, such a scheme would be unnatural and therefore an evil instead of a good.

It is impossible to define the *determining number* of any particular feature in society. But common sense easily enables us to judge whether the *determining number* has been arrived at, even though it be not precisely enumerated. For instance, if, in a small town of a thousand households, murder is committed in a hundred of them every year, we are right to regard that town as murderous. Although there is not a majority, to have so large a proportion of so exceptional a thing as murder is quite enough to determine the character of the town.

If, on the other hand, the thing of which we are talking is normal to man instead of being, like murder, abnormal, then we require a very large proportion to establish a determining number. Clothing is normal to man. If even a small proportion of the community go naked, the rightful determining number is not reached. Marriage is normal to man. You cannot say precisely out of a million adult men and women how many should be married in order to establish the institution of marriage as characteristic of that society but it may fairly be put at least a half: if only a fifth of the adult men and women in a community at any one time were married or had been married, we could fairly say that marriage was not an institution marking that community.

Now it is the same with the all-important institution of property, without which there can be no true citizenship and no full freedom. We cannot expect, however active we are in our reforms and however successful, to reach a society in which every single family, or every single adult individual, will own property: still less can we expect to reach a goal in which everyone owns property in an amount sufficient to secure complete freedom; but we can expect and should aim at setting a determining number of owners; and that will be a result sufficient for the normal working of a contented humanity. What the exact proportion may be no one could say, but common experience soon teaches us whether such and such a society is based on well-divided property, giving its tone to the whole community, and not defaced by exaggerated extremes of wealth and destitution. Denmark is such a society today, and the Catholic part of Ireland is rapidly becoming such a society. On the other hand, England is an extreme example of the opposite.

Next let this be remembered, that before we reach our aim of producing a determining number of owners, that is, of free men, you will have to pass through a stage in which the proportion is not yet that of the determining number, but is only pointing towards it. It is essential to envisage the gradual character of any change of this sort. We shall re-establish property by just laws and by good social and legal machinery for its erection and preservation, but we shall not re-establish it all at once; and any scheme proposing to do so bears the mark of futility and folly by so doing.

The change from a capitalist, that is, a proletarian society, to a society of free men owning the instruments of their livelihood, must come by successive steps of immaturity and peril, during which the old forces of competition and greed and insecurity will continually threaten its further advance. But having passed a certain stage it will continue to develop and to form more and more citizens in its own image. That is what happened when society was converted from the pagan to the Christian mood. Even when there were Christian emperors governing the world, the Christians were still a smaller body than their opponents. It took a full century for the tide to turn sufficiently for a majority to be present on the Christian side, counting together the East and the West. It took at least two centuries or more before the mass of men in the Roman Empire were Christian.

We must not hope to proceed very rapidly, although we shall need to strike root vigorously in the first stages of the affair. When a considerable body of economic freedom has been established, that body will demand laws preserving such freedom and further transforming capitalism into free conditions. What had been exceptional will become more and more normal in the eyes of onlookers; but the exceptions will survive. It is probably that, even when we have a society deeply colored by the institution of well-divided property, even when we have the great mass of families and individual owners of their means of livelihood and therefore free men, we shall still have attempts at re-starting capitalist experiments and we shall certainly have what is inevitable to all human movements, strong reactions impeding the advance of the good thing.

It is important to remember all this because nearly all those who come forward with false schemes for *finding a Way Out* of our present grievous troubles promise speedy, or even immediate, results, expect them, and therefore prepare men for inevitable discouragement.

No; the way we must set to work is the way in which every movement that has succeeded has gone to work. We must form "cells": we must make experiments in ownership, corporate and personal. We must go through a long period of preparation by argument and by making people familiar with the saving ideal of well-distributed property till they are no longer ready to tolerate the bad opposite of a few owners controlling a mass of non-owners. What is more, all such transitions involve continual compromise. Not compromise on principle, but on means of action. If, for instance, you were to sweep away the chain stores and the department stores in one moment, you would create masses of unemployment. If you were to restrict competition as fully as it should ideally be restricted and to impose such restrictions suddenly on the existing machinery of social life, there would be chaos. That is even true of the destruction of monopoly. Monopoly in private hands is all evil thing. Where it is unavoidable it must, as we shall see in a later article, be put into public hands. But if you were to strike suddenly at all existing monopolies, violently and without discrimination, you would certainly do more harm than good, and, what is more, you would probably ruin your chances of reform altogether. All this is by way of explanation, so that we may understand the task that is before us in seeking our escape from the economic misfortunes of the modern world.

Chapter Twenty-One

The Differential Tax

The first question which a practical man will ask of one who desires to restore private property is how are you going to do it without violence and injustice? At present, in the industrial world, the mass of those who produce do not own: they live on a wage. Even in the agricultural world most of those who used to be free men are caught in the mesh of usury, and are without institutions for maintaining their independence. How can you, without violence and injustice, change a state of society, however bad, which has crystallized so thoroughly, and is hard set in its mold? The answer to this main question is that the prime instrument for effecting the change is the Differential Tax.

The principle of the Differential Tax is that a different proportion of taxation, as well as a different amount, may be applied to men in different circumstances. For instance, if you apply an income tax of zero to incomes under $2,000, of 5 percent between $2,000 and $5,000, of 10 percent between $5,000 and so on, that is a differential tax. Or again, if you charge an amount of $5 for taking out one license for a particular purpose, $15 for taking out two licenses, $50 for taking out three, and so on, you are applying a differential tax to licenses.

There is nothing revolutionary today about the idea of the Differential Tax. We are all used to it and we all practice it. The trouble is that we do not practice it for the one really useful end it may serve, which is the better distribution of property. When a very rich man dies in England or in France today, half his property may go to the state, but the state does not use that windfall for the re-establishment, as owners, of men now destitute. It uses such capital sums to supplement its own income-expenditure. It spends the estate duties on salaries, social services, public works, and *not upon financing the re-establishment of the property* which is the one thing it ought to do in the case of a tax specially aimed against excessive accumulation.

The ways in which Differential Tax can be used to re-establish private property in the mass of men are various, according to the form of evil attacked. One obvious and primary way is to establish a Differential Tax upon the passage of property by sale: make it easier for the poor man to buy and the rich man to sell. Such a principle, applied to agricultural land, has already had excellent effects on certain parts of Europe, where the soil had fallen into few hands. When large property buys up small, let the tax be heavy. When small property buys fragments of large property and so helps to divide up property, let the tax be light and at last non-existent. In the same way Differential Tax can help to eliminate gradually — and, what is more important, to check at source — the growth of exaggerated distributing centers, big departmental stores and chain stores. The state grants a license, for instance, for the sale of tobacco. It makes that license cheap for the small man who runs a tobacco store, and more and more expensive for the big store which only makes tobacco one of the items among the innumerable ones it sells. The state taxes the individual business such and such an amount. When a chain starts in several towns, or in many places of the same large town, let each store in that chain be taxed progressively higher as the number of the stores in the chain increases until, at a certain limit, the tax makes the growth of chain stores impossible.

The same principle would apply to financial corporations, the tax falling in inverse proportion to the number of their bona fide members. A similar principle could be applied to one of the most powerful instruments for concentrating property in few hands, I mean advertisement. A certain area of advertisement, a certain frequency of repetition, paying so much, let any abnormal increase thereof pay a larger sum. I have cited elsewhere the French tax which levies a few cents on every hoarding, but fails to distinguish between a sky sign as big as a house and a placard hung outside a window. There is no department of economic activity to which this principle of the Differential Tax cannot be applied. It may be just or necessary to limit the amount of a novel differential tax to new developments; to let, for instance, the large advertiser already possessed of certain spaces for this activities retain them without extra cost. The value or necessity of working gradually applies here as it does to everything. But let the principle be fairly stated, rendered familiar and maintained. Until quite recently, in the development of modern capitalism, the Differential Tax has not been applied at all save for the purpose of revenue, never for the purpose of construction. Now it is precisely for the purpose of construction that the Differential Tax is most valuable. It is especially valuable in the region of sale of property.

But the principle carries with it a corollary which must not be shirked. We cannot apply the Differential Tax unless we have assessments of property. In very many countries such assessments are already the rule. Quinquennial assessments, for instance, showing the amount held by each citizen or family or business, every five years, provide a basis for a just application of the Differential Tax to the sale and purchase of real estate.

A man with an assessment of X dollars' worth of real estate is in negotiation with a man with a quinquennial assessment of 10 (X) dollars. If the small man sells to the larger man let the bargain carry a tax of so much, but if the small man buys from the larger man let the transfer carry only half as much tax. This principle underlay the very wise provisions of the late Mr. Gregory Wyndham's great Land Act for Ireland. It took an imperfect form, a bonus being offered by the large man to the small man, but the underlying idea is sound, for the underlying idea is to break up the great estates and increase the number of small ones.

There are two arguments against the use of the Differential Tax, arguments frequently repeated and of considerable weight — but not conclusive. The first argument is directed against the complexity of such a scheme, the second is based upon the ease of evading the tax.

The answer to the first is that little novel machinery is required, nor any great added complexity to the existing fiscal arrangements of most countries. Thus, when it was argued recently in England that the Differential Tax on the sales of land would require widespread and detailed investigation into values and situation, it was at once answered that the Treasury was already in possession of the information. Under what is called Schedule A of the English Income Tax the Treasury knows every year what value of real estate is in the hands of what citizens. The figures are not published but they exist.

As to evasion, that is a point which is repeated whenever any new tax is proposed. Obviously some taxes are easier to evade than others. The income tax and estate duty perhaps the easiest of all. But no evasion will take place if the penalties for evasion are sufficiently severe and the conditions sufficiently defined. Moreover the evasion of the Differential Tax in the great majority of cases is difficult. If the chain stores be registered under various names, those cannot be unknown to the taxing authority, and what is more, the use of various false names would destroy half the efficacy of the chain. The department store cannot conceal the number of its departments and under a license system could not sell anything unknown to the taxing authorities. One fixed principle must certainly be maintained and will be the hardest of all to maintain, under the severe fiscal pressure which modern States suffer. That is the principle of earmarking the product of the Differential Tax for the purpose of starting the better distribution of property: for financing the same, for the granting of bonuses, for the founding of guaranteed corporations and the rest. The Differential Tax has a chief function to perform in the disintegrating of large accumulations and the consequent fostering of small accumulations. It has also a secondary task to perform, which is the allocation of its receipts to the main purpose of the whole scheme. In both cases it is a necessary instrument for the wider distribution of property which should be the aim of all sound social reform today.

Chapter Twenty-Two

The Guild System

The guild is the oldest, most necessary, most deeply rooted of all human institutions. It has appeared in all civilizations which are at all stable, because it is necessary to stability. It has flourished especially at a time when our race was agreed upon a common religion and had a common high civilization. It only disappeared comparatively recently. We shall be compelled to restore it if we are to enjoy freedom at all, and the sooner we do so on the right lines the better. It will be especially valuable in the industrial field, which is that part of human life which most needs setting right today. The guild is essentially this — *An association of men engaged in the same occupation, and its primary object is mutual support.* These general terms involve a number of particular ones, which we have today mainly forgotten, and which we must recall if we are to restore property and make it stable and permanent — which is the condition for restoring freedom and human dignity and the family, all of which industrial capitalism has so grievously wounded. The detailed functions which the guild performs, apart from its general function of mutual support and guarantee among men of a similar craft, are as follows:

First; it guarantees their property. It does not destroy it as communism would do; it does the exact contrary. It makes property permanent and sees to it that undue competition and hostile action between the various members shall not lead to the eating up of the poorer man by the richer man. Thus, of the very first activities of the guild which we discover in full use for hundreds of years, is the making of laws for the conduct members, and the making of those laws so that each member may continue to be, within certain limits, a free member of the guild and a free owner of his own means of livelihood. The guild does not prevent the industrious man from flourishing, nor set a premium on idleness or inefficiency, but it makes rules whereby entrance into the guild is only to be obtained on certain conditions, whereby there is a term of probation before a man becomes a full member, whereby those who desire to work in such and such a craft must belong to the guild and whereby undue competition is checked.

Second; the guild has by charter from the state the right to deal with the matters which are the occupation of its members, and the right to such occupation is restricted to members of the guild; but the state does not allow the guild to exclude willing workers, still less to sell the privilege of membership. Entry to it must be open to all upon a sufficient test of efficiency in the trade concerned.

Third; a guild member must observe in his competition against others guildsmen of his own craft cetain limits. There are things he may do and things he may not do. There are rules for his professional conduct which he must obey under penalty of being turned out of the guild and thereby losing his livelihood, and these rules are designed for two main objects, the good working of the craft and the maintaining of its members, so that each, with a certain minimum of industry and efficiency, is certain of a livelihood.

Fourth; the guild is self-governing within the limits of its charter, the charter granted to it by the public authority of the state.

The way in which the guild works when it is in full life we can only study nowadays from the documents of the past — and they should help u to restore the guild today. But we get clear ideas of it from the relics of guild action in the little that remains of the old guilds. We see it in some degree among lawyers and still more among doctors, especially in old European countries. Thus, even in England, highly capitalist though England is, a man is forbidden to practice as a doctor unless he has proved, under examination and by medical practice during a time of probation, his ability to exercise that trade. In many places a doctor is, by the rules of his society, forbidden to advertise, A doctor, by the customs of his society — which have the force of law, for he cannot break them without losing his place in the corporation — does not take a patient out of a colleague's hands without that colleague's leave. A doctor is bound to preserve certain rules of honor and discretion in connection with his profession which are virtually guaranteed by the guild of which he is a member.

What is here true of the medical profession used to be true of all activities in the state.

The corporate union of the guilds guaranteed the independence of each member. The right working of the craft in which he was engaged and the restriction of competition within reasonable limits were assured. Its general effect was to prevent the undue enrichment of one member at the expense of others, and though the rules were elastic and the margin for differences in earning corresponding to differences in talent and opportunity was wide, the guild was the safeguard of continued property and independence. The spirit of the guild, even if the name guild be not used, applies to much else than productive crafts or learned professions. It applies to agriculture in the shape of co-operative institutions for the village and of guarantees against the absorption of the land into too few hands. It applies to distribution, and it applies to transport. In distribution today the guild would be especially valuable; it would check competition and guarantee the small man his livelihood and preserve the better customs of the trade: protecting the public against adulteration of goods, against scamped work and against deficiency of all kinds.

The guild, to be serviceable to a great state, must be subdivided. There may be any number of local guilds, but they must have some common bond, just as trade unions have today. (Trade unions resemble a guild in a sort of imperfect way. They do not guarantee property; on the contrary, they were invented to protect the proletariat against a minority of owners and they are concerned with the limiting of production instead of the excellence of it; but they got their spirit of co-operation and of checking competition from the traditions of the guild.)

We shall do nothing toward the restoration of property unless we also re-establish the guild. And we must apply the principle of the guild to every kind of human activity in order to stabilize and to guarantee property; and, with property, independence, in order to make the labor of every man worth the laborer's while. We can make of the guild the co-operative owner of great undertakings which require such co-operation; we can make it the protector of the small owner, of the small owner of one store, for instance, and of the owner of individual shares in a large store where many distributors work together. Every kind of good would flow from the re-establishment of the guild, and without the re-establishment of the guild the effort to maintain well-distributed property, even if we had already achieved that good distribution, would be vain; for the guild alone can guarantee the permanence of well-distributed property. But there is one obstacle to the founding of guilds. There is one rock upon which any attempt to restore the guild may be shipwrecked. Until we have learned to avoid this obstacle or to blast it out of the way the restoration of property cannot be secured. that obstacle is the foolish and irrational principle of unlimited competition. The whole spirit of the guild is opposed to that idea. The guild, one might almost say, comes into existence, and has always come into existence, with the object of preventing men from being destroyed by the demon of unrestricted competition, which is only another word for unrestricted greed. So long as men confuse freedom with the abuse of freedom in this form, so long will not only the guild, but property, to maintain which the guild exists, remain unattainable. Men must be accustomed to the idea of a limited society with the privilege of exercising this or that function, open to all (but only under the condition of accepting guild membership) before our effort at the restoration of property can be begun. Perhaps the revival of an idea to which men have grown so unaccustomed will be the hardest part of our task. Yet, unless we succeed in that task we must despair of that very liberty the name of which may be used by our opponents for defeating our efforts. Without property, held by the mass of citizens — by a determining number of citizens — there is no freedom; and without the guild there is no permanent maintenance of property.

Chapter Twenty-Three

The Small Producer

The Free Man Working on His Own Land and Acting
Under Local Co-Operative Control as His Own Master,
Is the Corporate State's Program for the Farmer.
the Self-Governing Guild, Co-Operating with
Factory and Government, Is the Way Out for Labor.

It is imperative in the cause of civilization, that we save the small producer and the small distributor. I call him "small" in contrast to those huge agglomerations of capital which have bred communism and half the other evils of our time. But I do not use this word "small" to make him out an unimportant person. He is all-important to human society and, under a scheme of properly distributed property, though his property would not be large it would be sufficient for his independence, his dignity and the security of his livelihood.

At any rate the name does not matter. The point is that the individual farmer and craftsman — or rather he and his family, if he has one — should be fostered and preserved by society instead of being crushed under, as he has been under our recent insane social motives of mere greed and criminal competition.

Property, widely distributed in many hands (which would be the salvation of society today) does not, of course, only mean the small producer. It means also the small distributor or storekeeper (of whom I shall speak in my next article); it means also the small shareholder, the small owner of state bonds and the rest of it. But the small producer must be saved as soon as may be, and established on a firm basis if we are to save society and to establish social justice. For it is upon him always that a healthy state reposes.

He is of two kinds just mentioned: the farmer and the craftsman. The farmer owning his own land and his own implements of labor and his own stock is at the foundation of the agricultural side.

The craftsman owning the place in which he works, the tools with which he works, the house in which he lives and from which he sells his produce, was for centuries the foundation of the industrial side of life: in the right sense of that word "industrial." The small individual producer, carpenter, smith, etc., cannot be wholly restored, as the farmer can, for machinery has come in to make the great difference, but he can be in part restored (it is essential that he should be restored as much as possible), and acting cooperatively with his fellows he can also be made a shareholder of the larger enterprises where large and expensive machinery is necessary. To begin with the farmer: He is agricultural. He produces food and the raw material of clothing, essential necessaries of the human race. Nothing has yet replaced, or apparently can replace, the man working on the land with his family. Capitalism has made every effort to oust that man, to replace him by great accumulations of stock and great acreage under one control. Communism, the direct product of capitalism, and suffering from the same moral evils as capitalism — especially its inhumanity — has made similar attempts to put agriculture under bondage. These attempts have already in part broken down and will break down yet further. Both these bad things, capitalism and communism, can flourish in great cities through the factory and every other form of concentrated ownership by a few rich interests acting as masters over the mass of citizens.

But, for the production of food, and the necessaries for the raw material of human life, it still remains true that the family, based on its ownership of the land, is the best working unit. That unit has been wounded almost to death, but the wound can be healed, and the farmer on his own land can be restored. What is necessary to such a sane and good result?

Regulated and guaranteed co-operation are necessary. the farmer as an individual is, with his family, powerless in the face of unrestricted greed and competition and great masses of capital concentrated outside his control, especially the massed capital of bankers and lending corporations. To restore that control over his own land and life which was once the birthright of the farmer, we need co-operation in two forms. First for credit; secondly for marketing.

The farmer must be backed by *co-operative* credit: by local *co-operative* banks of which he is himself a member and which, in their turn, are backed by society as a whole; that is, by the state. The numbers in which farmers can best co-operate must be left to local circumstances. The connection between their co-operative credit, and the state which guarantees it must be left to negotiation and debate. But the root principle lies there. The farmer, when he needs credit, must have available a supply of credit *under the control of himself and his fellows:* credit, not as an enemy but as an ally. And he must have State-guarantee of such credit, so that his local co-operative credit association, excluding all other forms of credit, shall be stable and not open to destruction by outside rivals.

Next he must have co-operative marketing. But this can well be left voluntary because when men appreciate its advantages they come into it naturally and of their own accord. The Danish system is here the great example. It applies principally to dairy produce, but also applies to pretty well any agricultural produce. A central board, though it be only local and on a small scale, which can give advice, deal with goods in bulk and furnish the advantage of cheap agricultural machinery and the rest, is essential.

But more than that is essential. It is also essential that society, the state, or whatever you like to call it shall overlook the affair in some degree, and particularly shall be the guardian of the farmer against distant competition of which he knows nothing and which he can in no way control. It is also essential that just minimum prices for his produce shall be fixed and insisted upon and that he shall be fortified against underselling from outside.

That is how the new Corporate state ought to work, and could work, for the preservation of the oldest and best of human activities — the free man working on his own land, and acting under local co-operative control, as his own master.

Now as to the craftsman: the man who works with his own tools on his own premises.

You will hear it said that the small craftsman is doomed, that there is no chance of his standing up to the competition of large units of capital and expensive concentrations of machinery. That is false. The craftsman — that is, the carpenter, the smith, the maker of furniture and of footwear and all the rest of it — has been almost destroyed, but not quite. He has not been almost destroyed through any fate or necessity, but only because his enemies have been in control and their money power has been allowed to run riot.

He cannot play the same part in the social economy that the farmer can because *some* things are obviously so much better made (not only so much more quickly, but *better*) on a large scale that we cannot do without them.

It his here that there comes in the system of the guild. You must have the guild for the small individual family producer, to protect him and to insure his property, but you

LARGE SCALE &

GUILDS

need it especially, and necessarily, for conditions under which work is done on a large scale. There the real producer, the man who, with his own hands produces the wealth, must be a guildsman, an owning shareholder in the factory and one whose conditions of labor and marketing and the rest are in the hands of a self-governing guild, to which the factory is attached itself, in touch with the authority of the state.

There articles of mine are very short, therefore very condensed, and only indicate the large lines. But those are the lines on which the salvation of society is proceeding in Europe today and can be continued elsewhere.

When the system is fully organized, it is called "the corporate state." It needs no despotism, though despotism has been called in to help the battle against the money power elsewhere. *Free men can organize themselves and remain in touch with a central state power of which they are the creators and the members without danger of tyranny.*

For instance, it is by state authority that preference call be given to the shareholder in the guild, or better still that ownership of shares in the guild can be confined to members thereof alone. It is not difficult to frame laws whereby a man can obtain shares through co-operative credit in the activities of his life at a rate which defies the competition of outside capital. Let that be organized and the problem is solved.

Let us always remember that a large number of small craftsmen are good for society. They are fully free. They do better work in many things than large factories can and the goods they produce with personal care are often of more service than goods produced anonymously. The principle is clear, it has only to be emphasized and followed, for the individual craftsman to survive or to be restored in sufficiently large proportion to affect the character of all society and, where that is impossible, for the craftsman to work through the guild of which he is a member and which can withstand, with its credit and mutual assistance, all attack from outside. But society must guarantee the system. That, we shall come to see, is essential.

Chapter Twenty-Four

The Small Distributor

*The Chain Store, the Combine, the Monopoly —
All Have Squeezed the Small Merchant Until
His Freedom Is Lost. The Guild System, in a Corporate
State, Would Afford Him the Protection He Needs.*

The small distributor means the individual storekeeper and his family.

He has also been called "a doomed relic of the past." That phrase is as much nonsense in his case as in the case of the craftsman. He has *seemed* to be doomed simply because the unrestricted competition of large concentrated capital has so violently attacked him as *almost* to destroy him. But it is not in the nature of things at all. A control of those evil activities would restore the small distributor within a certain very large measure, and, as in the case of the craftsman, where he is not restored, co-operation can come in to leave individual shareholders in a guild, power of control over their own lives.

Remember that the small distributor, the individual store-keeper with his family, fills a function most useful, not only to society as a whole, but to the very trade in which he is engaged. His value in that trade, through the personal interest that he and his family take in their business, through the human relationships set up by that connection, is clear. One is better served by people one knows than by mere servants, mere hired men of an impersonal mass of capital with whom neither the consumer nor the producer has any relation. But the function to society performed by the small distributor is even more important than this personal function. The independence of the family is guaranteed, and that is the very health of the state. No doubt under modern conditions, with rapid transport of goods, extensive and immediate communication of information, and the rest, there is a tendency to concentration which must be considered and dealt with. You could not, at a stroke, replace the present system of highly centralized, impersonal distribution by distribution in the hands of individuals and their families. But where such concentration is necessary or unavoidable, you can again have the all-saving, salutary principle of the guild. And the machinery for establishing it is in licensing the carrying on of the diverse forms of trade. If the grocer must belong with his large store; if he is a guildsman shareholder in that store and if outside competition against his guild is forbidden, then he is no longer exploited. He is an owner and a free man. By a system of licensing you can establish the essential principle of differential advantage, giving easier conditions always to the individual or the family unit against the larger unit: make it more expensive, through the Differential Tax, for the large impersonal store to undersell the small man, at the same time restricting the right of trade to members of the grocers' guild.

Such a guild, making its own rules and protected by the general laws of the state which issues the license, supports and makes permanent the whole system of well-divided property in distribution.

Even as it is, under our present detestable system of unrestricted competition and huge irresponsible concentrations of capital, the small distributor is fighting hard to survive. The reason it is difficult for him to survive is not in the nature of things, but comes altogether from the allowing of the larger unit of capital to undersell, to beat down and to eliminate the smaller.

If we establish the corporate state and the guild system and apply it to distribution and production, the problem raised by our present diseased and moribund capitalist system is solved.

Here again co-operative credit will be necessary, just as we found it to be in the case of the individual or family producer. The distributor needs credit as much as the producer does. But let that credit be confined to co-operative banks, co-operative local systems of credit, closely connected with, and working with, the guild.

The guild, be it remembered, exercises jealous care over the undue extension of power in the hands of any one member thereof. It restricts competition after a certain limit, because it is concerned with the preservation of the individual owner of capital, of the individual storekeeper and his family; and, where there is a combination of these in one center, it preserves the continuity and stability of the individual shares in the combination.

The guild here, as everywhere, is the key to the whole affair: the guild guaranteed and supported by the state, enjoying the power to deal with its own activities and excluding outsiders — especially outsiders who come in as enemies and who desire to swallow up the dependent man and his family.

If it be asked how the corporate state would deal with the existing concentrations of capital in distribution, the answer is that we will deal with it by that universal principle of the Differential Tax, or differential preference, which applies here as it does to every other human activity. We must make it more difficult, by heavier taxation, for the impersonal, mere money power to hold distribution in its hands, and easier for the small man to establish his share. The small guildsman, applying for a license to trade in this and that, and in such and such a fashion, must be privileged against the existing, large combine. Nothing stands in the way but the habits inherited from the old, unrestricted competition, which is already breaking down and which has caused such untold misery.

I think I have already quoted in these articles (as I have repeated in many another place during my campaign of many years in favor of restoring property as an institution and the independence of the family and of the individual with it) the example of the tobacconist in England, the place from which I write. At any rate, if I am repeating that example it is worth repeating. It is most illuminating. In our country the tobacconists had established without legal guarantee, but by custom of their trade, a certain agreed margin of profit for each store that sold cigars, cigarettes, pipe tobacco, etc. the small man could live. The small tobacco store was flourishing everywhere. But its continued life and security depended, unfortunately, not on anything guaranteed by law, not on any established corporate state, but only upon general custom and agreement.

There came in a new combine of a few big tobacconists. Purchases were made on a larger and larger scale. Profits were cut down from the old agreed margin to a new, smaller margin upon which the small distributor of tobacco could not live. The usual excuse was advanced: "The new state of affairs made it cheaper for the consumer." But, the consumer in a healthy state is the mass of citizens, and that includes the tobacconist himself as well as everybody else. Kill the free, small dealer by this new, gigantic combine; turn him into a salaried agent with no property, and you afflict society in his case with that mortal disease which is everywhere destroying the freedom and security of the individual and of his family life.

The managers appointed by the new combine, managers on a competitive wage, and at the mercy of the new employers, took the place of the old, free and independent storekeepers. There followed, of course, arrangements between the new combine and the big wholesale monopolist vendors of tobacco, until at last that vague animal "the public" was compelled to take whatever it was offered by these two conspirators — the big distributing merger for retail stock, and the big vendors for tobacco wholesale. Today in England the storekeeper handling tobacco has become the hired servant (with no security, no property — nothing) of the combine, and the public gets, not what it wants, but what it is told to have — or go without.

Here as in everything else well-divided property is the flywheel which regulates the whole machine of economic freedom. When new mergers destroyed the small individual owner of property, freedom disappeared both at the consumer's end and at the distributor's end.

That is only one particular example. It only covers a comparatively small field of activity, but we have had the same thing over here in England in any number of other departments. The individual milk distributor has been swallowed up by the huge combine which is the master of the farmer who produces the milk as much as it is of the member of the unfortunate "public" who buys the milk, but buys it at the price fixed by the combine. With freedom there was choice and there was that vastly more important thing, the independence, security and happiness of the family engaged as units in the distribution of milk.

The moral is here as everywhere. Fight for and establish well-distributed property. Restore, bolster up and guarantee by corporate action the individual owners and their households. Have co-operative action at work by all means, but let it be in the hands of free men owning their proportion of the shares in the corporate thing.

Here again, as in every other case, you must have the corporate distributive function backed by public law. You must make it increasingly difficult, and at last impossible, for the combine to order the lives of men, who, from being free men, become their slaves.

Let no one say that this is a dream or, as the phrase goes "under modern conditions" impossible. Those so-called "modern conditions" are of our creation. They come from the application of a bad social philosophy, from the allowing of unrestricted greed to act at will, and from the neglect of the supreme truth that only citizens, economically free, can build up a healthy social state.

"MODERN CONDITIONS"

PRECLUDE

FREEDOM

Chapter Twenty-Five

The Functions of the State

The Socialists of Yesterday and the Communists of Today
Teach That Man Is the Slave of the State. But the State Exists
to Protect Man From Slavery — Slavery to Capitalism, or to
Itself. This Is the Function of the Democratic, Corporate State.

The state — that is, society as a whole — has a necessary and all-important function to perform when we shall have re-established a free and healthy society. We must recognize that function, we must not be afraid of it nor regard it as hostile to our endeavor.

The action of the state was so regarded as hostile to free-dom when it was put forward by those who were once called socialists and are nowadays called communists (it is all one). They — the communists, or socialists — proposed to make us slaves to the state, and human conscience revolted against so inhuman a conception.

The socialist of my youth — the communist of today — was and is often, and indeed usually, an academic sort of fellow, a bookish fellow, using formulas and quite out of touch with real life. He could see no "Way Out" of the abominations of industrial capitalism, which had ruined social life and denied social justice in all our great cities, save the substitution of state ownership for private ownership. One used often to hear his absurd contention that the more capital was concentrated in few hands the better for his ideal, because it would be the easier for the state to take over at last the private exaggerated profits of capitalist millionaires. That, as we know, has not come off. It cannot, in the nature of things, come off. You cannot bring about a good by fostering an evil. The big combinations of capital entrenched themselves and became more powerful than ever. The highbrow talk of a good time coming when they would be taken over by the state has melted into thin air. On the contrary, they became our masters, and now propose so to remain until they have destroyed right living.

No; we must not be afraid of state action where it is necessary. And we must lay down two principles which ought to be obvious and which can guide us throughout our reform.

These two principles flow from a certain primal principle which underlies them both. *We invoke the power of the state in order to prevent, not to encourage, enslavement to the state: we invoke the power of the state in order to re-establish well-divided property.*

From this primal principle derive two principles we must always remember in action as we proceed to the great reform. They are as follows: (a) Where monopoly is un-avoidable it must be directly controlled by, and is better in the hands of, society. (b) It is the function of the state to guarantee by its laws and authority the stability both of cor-porate and of individual ownership, and especially to protect that ownership against external attack, whether from foreign sources or from masses of concentrated capital hostile to private ownership.

As to (a):

Monopoly is sometimes unavoidable. The coming in of some machinery which is manifestly and overwhelmingly su-perior for production than an older, cheaper, and smaller form of machinery, does sometimes make monopoly inevi-table. It has already thus become inevitable, for instance, in certain forms of transport through the creation of the rail-road system. There are countries where competition of a healthful kind is still possible between distinct railroad cor-porations, but in all small countries and most large countries today railroad transport is virtually a monopoly. Why, then, that monopoly must be controlled; and, seeing that it con-cerns all men directly, had better be controlled directly by the state.

But this is emphatically not true of all modern monop-oly. A great mass of it is artificial — due to combines which are the product of greed. The small economic saving ef-fected by a combine of "overheads" is negligible compared with the loss of economic freedom which it entails and the consequent poisoning of society. The areas over which state monopoly must be exercised as a matter of necessity are restricted, they are not universal.

The tendency of officials to take over our, lives must be jealously watched, and they can be just as jealously watched today as they were of old, if we keep clearly before our eyes the universal principle that monopoly must never be let slip into the hands of state officials, save where monopoly is, of its nature, unavoidable. It is not unavoidable when it makes things or services slightly cheaper. It is not unavoidable because uniformity is better than local differences; on the contrary, uniformity is much worse. It is not unavoidable because Jones is a rather better man than Smith. It is quite easy for Jones and Smith to exist side by side if Jones' power of competition against Smith be limited by the guild.

Monopoly is not unavoidable save where, in the very nature of things, it cannot be avoided. Where that is the case you must have state control, or better, if it be possible, state ownership. But even then the principle of the guild applies, and the state can work with, and through, a corporate system of production or service, the shareholders in which are the men who themselves produce the wealth or the service.

Concerning (b):

The state is also there to guarantee the stability of well-distributed property when we have arrived at that goal, and even while we are only on our way to it. Unless laws exist which guarantee well-divided property against ruinous competition; unless laws exist which jealously watch the just price and punish underselling; unless laws exist which prevent the small man being destroyed by usury and which exclude the grabbing of credit by agencies over which the small man has no control, unless, in a word, laws exist to support the guild, to reinforce its power and to give to its freely made customs the force of law over its members, there is nothing doing.

It is, I repeat, the function of the state to prevent our becoming slaves, whether to the state itself, as mad communism proposes, or to nameless, impersonal, huge concentrations of money power — as we now actually are.

And the state is there also to prevent the coming in of forces from outside which may destroy the small man. Let us always remember that it was the merchant engaged in import and export, who could snap his fingers at the regulations of the guild at home make profits from abroad independently of the society in which he lived. He it was who began to break up the old state of affairs which governed our lives in Christendom when the guild was supreme — in better days than these.

For instance, the state is there to prevent foreign competition from destroying the small man at home. Here in England, where I write, the state could prevent the ruining of the farmer by goods produced under labor conditions intolerable to our society. The state is not there to protect individual capitalist profits, but it is there, and must be there, to protect corporate economic action within its boundaries.

In other words, you must have the action of the state, and even the powerful .action of the state, to guarantee that very freedom of well-divided property which is the one and only safeguard against slavery in some form — either to the state itself or to big capital.

The state is not the enemy of property. It is, in any rightly constituted society, the protector of property; not the special protector of large property; but the special protector of the system under which property is stable in many hands and in which men live together as free men, protected in the independence of themselves, their families and their posterity. To regard state action as merely hostile, is foolish. To regard it as unnecessary is ridiculous. The state *must* have power. The whole question is whether that power shall be directed towards the maintenance of our economic freedom or against it. There must be links between the power of the state and the local corporate associations; the guilds, which the state is there to maintain, to establish, to continue and to protect. These links are best devised by many free men acting through free association and debate; by putting the guilds into touch with state authority; by the guilds receiving their charters from the state and with their local knowledge informing the state and suggesting reforms and changes.

There is, I repeat, no sort of reason why such a system should be arbitrary and tyrannical. It can be voluntary and free. The corporate state has indeed appeared in arbitrary and tyrannical form elsewhere, but that was because, before it arose, society had been almost murdered by the spread of communism. If we take the thing in hand before the danger has grown to such proportions, there is nothing to prevent our having a corporate state powerful to guarantee economic freedom, but impotent to destroy it.

Summary and Conclusion

The Restoration of Well-Divided Property, and the Protection of Its Ownership by Guilds Under a Corporate State, Is the World's Alternative to the Quick Solution Through Communism — a Remedy That Would Be Worse Than the Disease.

Let us sum up the conclusions to which we have arrived.

The world today is sick of a mortal disease which we call industrial capitalism, but of which the true name is proletarianism.

Men politically free have lost their economic freedom. The citizen in the industrial world is economically enslaved. He finds his position more and more intolerable through insecurity and the lack of all prospects. He has nothing and is apparently debarred from ever having anything. He can live only as a wage-slave at the orders of others who have no moral authority over him, between whom and himself there is no human tie. *He is so placed merely because the instruments of his livelihood do not belong to him but to a minority who are his masters.*

153

That condition cannot endure. It is already breaking up. We must find some "Way Out." The troubles have come to apply not only to industrial conditions but to agricultural conditions as well, for the farmer is in the hands of the usurers, industrial capitalism having captured the instruments of credit. He can be relieved by forced action, by the arbitrary wiping out of debt; but that is not a permanent policy. There is nothing to prevent his falling again into the same miserable insecurity and destitution.

What is the Way Out?

The obvious Way Out, the line of least resistance, is communism, but that is no true solution, it is a remedy worse than the disease. It was born of capitalism, and continues the worst feature of capitalism, which is eating up humanity and leading to servitude.

The true *Way Out* is by the restoration of property. We must work for the establishment of a society in which a determining number of families shall be economically free. There is no possibility of economic freedom without property. The alternative is clear and inevitable. Restore property or restore slaver; whether it is to be slavery in the form of slavery to the state and its officials, or slavery to individuals matters nothing, save that the latter is perhaps the less inhuman. The only alternative to the tendency to slavery first, and at last to barbarism, to the extinction of our civilization, is to re-establish property, and with it the freedom and well-being of the family.

The instrument whereby well-distributed property may be restored is the Differential Tax. It needs no revolutionary

HUMANLY INTOLERABLE

legislation. We have it with us already. All it needs is its proper application. The Differential Tax should be used for the purchase of property for the destitute, for their establishment as owners and for the dislocation of the present vast accumulations of property in few hands. There is no necessity to aim at economic equality. It is not even advisable. It is not *some* difference in fortune that men find intolerable. What men find intolerable is destitution and their consequent subjection to other men and exploitation by them. What men find intolerable is the arbitrary subjection to another's will.

That property can be restored, and with it the dignity and freedom of the family is certain; but the effort will be useless unless we make the fruit of it permanent. Well-divided property, a society the tone of which is everywhere given by the presence of owners in a determining number, is within our grasp. A simple general policy would suffice to create it: gradually, of course, but certainly. It is no use, however, working on these lines unless property, when it shall have been restored to the many, shall be rendered stable.

The institution necessary for rendering well-divided property stable is the guild. In the place of impersonal and uncontrolled competition we must establish the rules and organization of the guild: the corporate state.

By the guild we can re-create and defend the independent farmer, the independent craftsman, the independent distributor. The guild cannot arise in a madly competitive society dominated by vast units of concentrated capital unless it be protected under a charter from the state. Its powers of self-government, its rules for production, distribution and exchange — rules framed by, and obeyed by, its own members — must be guaranteed by public charter.

Further, there must be links between the general authority of the state and the authority of the guild. We must have the guild, not only in production, distribution and exchange, guaranteeing the livelihood and independence of citizens who are also owners, we must have the guild in the operation of credit as well. Credit must be co-operative if well-divided property is to be secure. The institutions controlling credit, separate from the interests of those to whom such credit is extended, are tyrannical institutions; they make of credit an instrument of prey.

The guild everywhere — the very opposite of communism and the great means of escape from communism — is the watchword. There is but one exception. Certain inevitable monopolies and public functions must be under public ownership and control. The economic power of the state must be admitted for the very purpose of establishing economic freedom of the citizens and their families. The authority of the state is necessary for the maintenance of corporate industry and the corporate rules governing and securing agriculture as well.

There you have the corporate state and the restoration of freedom: a society of free men.

Such a society can be built if its principles are clearly explained and put into action. Its beginnings can be founded at once; and of their own strength they will grow.

SUMMARY AND CONCLUSION

We must not expect, and we cannot attain, a perfect state. We must not expect, and we cannot attain immediate universal results. There must be growth, and growth is of its nature gradual. But if we start upon these right lines, those who are now young will live through a world the freedom and prosperity of which will continually increase; in one human lifetime at least, probably less, the corporate state, founded on secure, well-divided ownership, could be fully established and in being.

It is rare indeed in human affairs that a happy society can be formed and maintained. However well it be planned, and however thoroughly the plan may be carried out, the imperfections and vice of man's fallen nature — especially greed — are always present to menace the good thing. But at least we can know our goal and aim at it and follow on the right lines towards it. The Way Out is not imaginary and impracticable; the citizen owning property securely, and thereby living a free life, has stood in the past for generations, and may stand again. But such well-being in the past has always been accompanied by corporate economic institutions safeguarding the individual and the family and maintaining property by mutual assistance and by the authority of society. Not the perfect state, but the good state, is attainable. The way to it is clear. All that is needed is the widespread explanation of the way and the continuous will to pursue our object to its triumph.

Our aim, then, is clear, and our goal is clear. The two main obstacles before us are equally clear.

THE WAY OUT

The first obstacle is the existing proletarian mind, which has forgotten, or is beginning to forget, what economic freedom means, who sees it in terms of wages only. To convert the proletarian mind to the idea of property, to make men so long subject to proletarian conditions understand the necessity of property and to understand that freedom must be restored, is a hard task, and the difficulty of such a task is the first obstacle we have to meet.

The second obstacle is the temptation offered by rapid methods of escape; of which the most obvious, and therefore the most perilous, is communism. If we follow the line of least resistance towards communism we shall end, not in the establishment of the good state and of a tolerable human life, but in disaster, leading to ultimate servitude. To build up, to establish, to make certain, a good thing is always a greater effort than that demanded for palliatives and immediate remedies. The effort to restore makes on us demands not only for patience, but for energy and for continuous sacrifice. But the reward, if we reach our goal, will be a human society consonant to the nature of man, his free will and his rational expectation of happiness even in this unhappy world.

Panis Humanus. Right-living. Our daily bread, of the body and of the soul.

Catholic Authors Press

Catholic Authors Press is dedicated to promoting preserving our rich Roman Catholic literary heritage. Catholic Authors does this through the rescue and recirculation of used and out-of-print books as well as the publishing of rare and classic titles from the past for the next generation of faithful. Catholic Authors maintains a comprehensive biographical database of Catholic writers accessible online for free and plans to offer workshops for young and aspiring Catholic writers in answer to the plea of Pope Pius XI: "In vain do you build schools and churches if at the same time you do not also build up a good Catholic literature."

CPSIA information can be obtained
at www.ICGtesting.com
Printed in the USA
BVHW032140250719
554421BV00001B/19/P